Jan

RAISING UP BOYS IN KANSAS

Short Stories of Misfits, Hicks and Stubble Bums
Learning About Life

Published by James Grennan

This book is dedicated to my mother, Maxine,
who did her best to raise seven children.

"I was born and raised in Kansas. The worst things are the locusts, mosquitos, the flatness, the humidity. The greatest things are the simplicity of life, watching the thunderheads building on the horizon, and running through cornfields."

Erin Brockovich

Contents

Contents

Contents

Contents

Introduction

I was born in Concordia, Kansas, and raised in Jamestown, Kansas. Jamestown is located in north central Kansas, 11 miles west of Concordia, and is primarily an agricultural community of approximately 300 people. Our family lived in town and rented farm land where we raised wheat and milo. My father, John, was proud to be 100% Irish. He had a propensity for alcohol, and he was quite a poker player. My mother, Maxine, while raising seven children, took in washing for some of the old people around town. I had two brothers and two sisters older than me, and one sister and one brother younger than me. My dad, my brothers and I did custom combining during the summer wheat harvest all over the Midwest from Texas to Montana for over 20 years. I helped with that effort for almost 10 of those years. The family farmed rented ground, and my dad had a grain hauling business, as well. The ground we farmed was nothing but gumbo, rocks, ditches and bindweed. These stories are my memories of my childhood, and are compiled from the time I was old enough to remember until my mid-twenties, when I left Kansas. Whenever I talked about my childhood to my friends and acquaintances, many of them said, "Jim, you should write a book! I really enjoyed listening to that story!" So, here it is. If you grew up in rural America, you will probably relate to one or more of these stories. I hope you enjoy them. Jim

***

According to Roget's 21st Century Thesaurus, Third Edition, synonyms for misfit are:

Dissenter
Dropout
Eccentric
Freak
Oddball
Outsider
Weirdo
Demonstrator
Nonconformist
Protester
Radical
Beatnik
Individualist
Loser
Offbeat
Different breed
Lone wolf
Odd man out

Growing up, I felt that I could have been labeled any of them.

RAISING UP BOYS IN KANSAS

Not Broke with Two Silver Dollars

Growing up in Kansas in the '50s was a lot like growing up in the '30s. The drought was so severe. Crops were always short, hardly amounted to anything. Money was real tight in north central Kansas. Most people didn't have a pot to pee in or a window to throw it out of.

The first thing I remember when I was very young, my mother gave my younger brother and me a bath in the kitchen sink. I was a year older than him, so I got one half of the sink and he got the other half. Talk was going around that people were going to start losing their homes. I remember asking my mom if we were going to have to move out of our house.

She said, "No, look in that window sill there."

So I did, and there were two silver dollars.

She said, "As long as we have those two silver dollars, we're not broke. So quit worrying."

"The farmer is the only man in our economy who buys everything at retail, sells everything at wholesale, and pays the freight both ways." John F. Kennedy

1

The Plastic Chicken Scam

When I was about 3 or 4, I was out playing by the road, the main road, up the hill by our house. Here comes this kid about my age down the hill. He had in his hand a plastic chicken and when he pushed down on the chicken's head, out popped a little colored egg. I said to myself, I've got to have that. That's something I've got to have.

I asked him what kind of a trade he'd make for that plastic chicken. He said, "Well, you probably have a pocket knife, don't you?"

And I said, "Yeah, I do."

"Maybe I'll trade you this chicken for that pocket knife."

I went inside the house, got my pocket knife and came back out.

He looked it over and said, "Yeah, I believe I'll trade you this chicken for that pocket knife."

I said, "Okay, you've got a deal."

He took my pocket knife, put it in his pocket and said, "You know, I'm going to have to go home and make sure this is all right with my folks, you know, trading this chicken for your knife." I thought, oh, okay. I was a little reluctant, but I agreed.

He took my pocket knife and the chicken and headed on home. That was the last I ever saw of my pocket knife, or the chicken. I should have learned a lesson back then that you can't just really trust everybody, but no, I didn't learn it and it's been a real problem for me down through the years.

Pigeon Eggs in Mom's Oven

When we were kids, we always had pet rabbits, pet pigeons, pet dogs, pet pigs, you name it and we had them. I don't remember what we did with the rabbits. They probably died of old age because they were pets. The pigeons, they liked to fly up and build their nests in the gutter. One summer there came about a four-inch gulley washer, and I looked up there and there was this poor pigeon sitting on her eggs in the water. I crawled around, got up there, put her on the porch roof and took her eggs out of the nest in the water. I thought to myself, those eggs aren't going to hatch in the water, so I asked my mom if I could stick them in the oven and turn the oven on low.

She kind of looked at me and probably had it all figured out that this was not going to work, but she let me do it. So I did. After a couple of days I could have had hard boiled eggs, probably, and of course, those eggs never hatched into any little pigeons either. Boy was I heartbroken.

Neighborhood Girl Scare

About the time I was 4, maybe 5 years old at the most, my mom came up to me and said that the lady up to the top of the hill had her little granddaughter visiting her for the summer and she needed to have someone as a playmate. I said it would be okay, but I wasn't much into girls then.

I went up there and knocked on the old lady's door and stood there waiting for somebody to answer the door. Over to my left, right off the porch, I heard the bushes rattling. I thought, I wonder what that's all about. All of a sudden this little girl jumped out of those bushes stark naked.

She said, "Come and get it if you want it." It scared the you-know-what out of me.

I went running home as fast as I could. I told my mother what happened.

She says, "Well, Jim, I don't think you have to claim her as one of your playmates this summer." Wow, was I relieved.

Learning the Consequences of My Actions

One winter day when I was in the first grade, snow and ice had built up on the soles of my shoes. When I went in to my class I used my shoes as ice skates and skated across the classroom floor. The music teacher was not impressed, to say the least. He gave me a good scolding and grounded me.

The next day, I thought I'd get back at the whole school system. So I took a handful of sand and small rocks and pitched them into the exhaust fan at the ground level boys' locker room. I can still hear those rocks hitting those fan blades.

Next thing I know, I'm sitting in the Principal's office, writing 100 times "I will not ever throw rocks in the exhaust fan again." At a very young age, I learned the hard way that there are usually consequences for bad behavior. Unless you're willing to do the time, don't do the crime!

"Working with family makes what you do worthwhile, as you teach kids responsibility and the importance of life." John Devos

Kite Flying Under Siege

I remember the end of winter, in February we'd make kites out of paper grocery bags, a couple of sticks, glue, and a little string. We couldn't afford a 10 cent kite at the store, so we'd make our own kites. I'd tell my mom, "Mom, it's time to fly kites," but she said, "No, Jim. I've got a rule that there's going to be no kite flying until at least the first day of March. February's still too cold."

So, that last week of February seemed like a month long, but along come the first of March. I couldn't wait to get out in the wheat field to the south, and get my kite up and see how high I could get it. I'd take some toilet paper and let the wind blow that toilet paper pretty high up on the string. The toilet paper served as make-shift parachutes. Then, I'd start shaking the string and watch that toilet paper come floating down, and boy, was that a thrill!

But, as luck would have it, after about three or four days of kite flying, some of the guys from the high schools would get wind of me flying my kite. One day in particular, I looked over my shoulder and here came about four high school kids with their bow and arrows. The next thing I know, they're standing under my kite, shooting their arrows up at the kite. Every once in a while one of them would hit my kite and bring it down. So I had to always watch over my shoulder to see if any of them were coming. When I saw them coming, I'd start reeling my kite in as fast as I could.

Church Stories

Before I started school, my mother became seriously ill and had to be hospitalized in Salina. With seven children and an alcoholic husband, my uncle agreed to take me and my little brother to his house. He lived about thirty miles down the road in a little town called Delphos. He was a Catholic Priest.

The first night, we were getting ready for bed, he said, "You boys need to go brush your teeth."

I told him, "I don't own a toothbrush, so I'll just borrow yours." I remember the look he gave me. I'll never forget that look.

So, he said to my brother and me, "Just take a little toothpaste and rub it on your teeth and we'll call it good!"

Next morning, he had a 7 o'clock Mass. He had my little brother and I serve at the mass as altar boys. We went into the church. I remember the church was kind of cold and dark, darker than normal churches. There were only three old ladies sitting in the front pew. We went into the back. He tried to find some altar clothes to fit and they were all too big to fit us, so he said. "We'll make it work. You boys can just wear the clothes you have on."

He then taught us how to ring the bell. Of course I was older, so I was in charge of ringing the bell and he said, "Now if you see me putting my hand down and there are two fingers out, ring the bell twice. If there's one finger, ring it once." I didn't think that was too complicated. I was sitting there watching him and all of a sudden, his hand drops. I couldn't see well enough and I thought, well, I can't tell if it's a one or two, so I lit up the church with the bell. He turned around and looked at me like, why are you ringing the bell? Well, I didn't know what I was supposed to do, but I didn't want to take a chance of not ringing that bell.

Pretty soon his hand dropped again, I couldn't tell if it was one finger or two, so I lit the church up with those bells again. He turned around and motioned me with his hand, and I didn't know, maybe he wants me to ring the bells again. So I lit up the church again. This happened 15 to 20 times, I suppose. To this day, if he's at a family reunion or gathering of any kind, he likes to tell that story about how the nephews just lit up the church with the bells non-stop it seemed like to him. He always has a really good laugh telling that story!

Never forget the time I was in church, probably 4 or 5 years old and the preacher, he said we needed to go out and evangelize a little bit, and maybe even bring somebody to church with us. I thought, well, I know just the kid. He needs a little church time. I asked him if he wanted to go to church with me that next Sunday. He was the same kid that beat me out of my pocket knife. He was pretty reluctant, but he agreed to go. So I brought him to church and about half way through the service, he just got up and walked out of the church. I thought, well, I guess he really doesn't want to be here. About a week later, probably the next Sunday, I go to church and two of the stained glass windows were broken. Somebody had thrown a rock through them. I thought I probably knew who that was. Of course, three or four people gave me a funny look when I was leaving church. I guess they probably had an inkling what young man did it, too. Needless to say, I never invited him back again.

One time I was in the church choir, there in my home town, and my aunt was choir director. We'd go practice our songs on, probably, Wednesday nights. I'm up there in the choir loft and I was only 7 or 8 years old. Sure sounded to me like everybody was singing off tune just a little, so I thought, well, you know, I'm just going to sing a little louder and maybe drown them out and that way it'll all work out. Well, next day or two, my aunt stopped me and said, "Jim, I don't want you to come to choir any more. You just don't have the voice for this." I thought, yeah, maybe I was the one that was off key a little bit.

"There are two spiritual dangers in not owning a farm. One is the danger of supposing that breakfast comes from the grocery, and the other that heat comes from the furnace." Aldo Leopold

That Branch Just Isn't Big Enough

When I was young and would get in trouble with my dad, he would always hand me his pocket knife and tell me to go out and cut a branch off the "switch tree." We had a bush in the back yard that had these branches that grew up and out of the ground. One time, I went out and found a small branch, cut it off, and brought it back in to him. He took one look at it and then said, "No, Jim. This branch is way too small. Go back out and cut me a bigger one." So, I went back out, cut a bigger one, brought it back in, and he proceeded to switch my behind a little with it. Oh, well. I thought it was worth a try.

Little Brother Finally Catches On

Once in a while, somebody would give me a candy bar. My little brother and I would always have to share it. I'd always break it in half and I'd give him the littler half, of course. Finally, he got wise to that. He said, "Jim, why don't you go ahead and keep breaking those candy bars in half and then let me decide which half I want." He figured out how to keep me from always getting the bigger half!

Playing Baseball with the Older Boys

When I was probably 5 or 6 years old, I was a Little League baseball player. My mother would cut out red Js and sew them on to our white T-shirts so we would have our own uniforms. Towards the end of the season, I was recruited by my older brother's team because they were running short of players. The coach told me to squat down in the batting box as low as I could and was told to never swing my bat. I was usually walked on four straight pitches. My brother's team ended up winning the tournament and everyone was real proud of me for always getting on base.

All was fine and well until the losing team checked on how old I was, and found out I wasn't old enough to be playing in their league. So the tournament was awarded to the team we defeated. Guess who all of the members of my brother's team blamed? Three guesses and the first two don't count.

Older Brother

I'll never forget the times I was up in the upstairs boys' bedroom. There were four of us boys that slept in this one little bedroom. My younger brother, Kevin, and I shared a bed. I always drew an imaginary line in the middle of the bed and told him, "Now don't you cross over that imaginary line." Every once in a while he would, and I'd tell him and push him back over on his side.

One night, my older brother was trying to get some sleep and he didn't like hearing us whispering or talking, so he would holler out, "The next time I hear talking or whispering, I'm going to throw a boot over there." Of course, it was pitch dark so, being young boys, my brother and I, we'd have to whisper, and all of a sudden, here comes a boot flying across the room and landed in our bed. I don't remember ever really getting hurt, but it was part of growing up with him because it happened multiple times.

My big brother, he was, I don't know why, but he was always kind of a bully to me. I know one time I had a half dollar. Of course back then all the money was made out of silver. We were upstairs and he said, "You need to give me that half dollar." I said, "No, I've worked for that. It's mine and you're not getting it." He said, "Well, I'm going to take it from you then." I told him, "I'll tell you what I'm going to do. I'm going to pull the top off of the staircase post, and I'll drop it in there. I'd rather see it go down there than for you to have it." He kept coming closer and so that's what I did. I removed the cap and dropped that money down inside that post. At least that kept him from having it!

One night in my late teens, while sitting down at the pool hall I told a drinking buddy of mine about dropping that half dollar down the stair post. He said to me, "Let's go up to your house and get it out." We pried the bottom off the stair case post and the half dollar was no longer there. Oh, well.

While we were on a roll, we took the wooden face off the fireplace thinking someone might have stashed something of value behind it. All

Dad and children greasing the one way
L-R: Johanna, Helen, Dad, Ace, Mary Jo, Teresa, Jim, Susie

that we found was a small paper airplane. I always suspected my brother of beating us to retrieving the half dollar.

After all those years of knowing my brother got the half dollar, my little sister, Helen, confessed to me that shortly after I dropped it into the stair post, she rigged up a yard stick with a glob of tape on the end of it and was able to fish it out. At a family gathering a few years ago, I told my brother about taking the stair post and the fireplace apart. All he had to say about it was, "Did you find my paper airplane?" Before we put the wooden face back on the fireplace, I took about 30 pennies and stashed them behind the fireplace. I didn't want the next treasure hunter to come away totally empty.

I remember one time during the summer when he and his buddy got me down in the grass and filled my mouth with a handful of "Pop Bugs." Once they let me up, I had a darn time trying to get them all out of my mouth.

I remember the time I got home from school. I was probably in the first grade. I went out to ride my little pedal pusher car and found that all four wheels were gone! My brother had taken the wheels off of it to make a homemade wooden Go Cart for himself. Boy was I mad! It was all just a part of growing up.

We had a real tiny, tiny closet, with a little door on it, under the stairs. One time, I was in the closet playing and all of a sudden the door closed. It was dark, real dark in there and I was hollering. Well, he thought it was funny so he just put a chair in front of the door knob so I couldn't get out. I was terrified and screaming at the top of my lungs and could hardly breathe. Next thing I know, he went in and got a towel and put that across the bottom of the door to keep any light or air at all from getting in there. Terrified me big time! After several minutes (seemed like an hour), he opened the door.

We'd all sit down to supper and mom fixed what she always figured would be enough to fill up her three girls, four boys, herself and dad. After everybody finished eating, she would walk in from the kitchen and say, "Did everybody get enough to eat?" Of course, everybody was still a little hungry, and she said, "Well, I'll go ahead and make another pan of biscuits." So she would, and she'd bring them in and we'd start passing them around. My brother, he'd take his table knife and smack me in the hand if I tried to grab one of them. I probably still have scars on my hands from that. Most every Sunday, mom would usually make fried chicken. That old song, Chicken Every Sunday, by Bobby Bare, comes to mind. Always makes me remember those Sunday chicken meals.

In the evenings, my brother used to pop up a big bowl of popcorn and put it in his lap while he sat in the rocking chair and read the newspaper. We used to walk by and grab us a hand full of his popcorn. He got real tired of that so he started putting a page of his newspaper over the bowl so he would hear us helping ourselves to his popcorn. To protect his property (so to speak), he would have a butcher knife at the ready just in case we didn't think he was serious. This put a stop to us taking any more of his popcorn.

One day walking home from school I looked up at the water tower and read the name of my brother and his two buddies, Del and Bill, painted in black on the water tower. At the time, all I could think of was how that would be a black mark on me since I was related to him. The three of them got in to trouble big time for that prank. I would have to say that being a hick just seems to run in the family, so to speak.

Another time he came home late one night all bummed out after he and a couple of his buddies tore the bumper of the car off trying to spring an old drunk out of the city jail by wrapping a long chain around the bars of the window at the jail. Seems as if the window's bars were stronger than the bumper. Oh, well. At least they gave it the old college try.

Sacking Potatoes to Pay Off Candy Debt

I remember the first job I ever had. My mother got me a job at the local grocery store, sacking potatoes. I had to take potatoes out of 100-lb gunny sacks and put them in 5-lb little totes, they used to call them. I know the reason my mother got me that job was because one time, when I didn't think anybody was looking, I was going down the candy aisle, and proceeded to fill my pockets full of candy. That wasn't a very smart thing, or a smart move on my part, but it happened. So my mother got me this job to help pay off the candy that I didn't pay for.

The worst part of the job was that sometimes I would stick my hand into a rotten potato and the smell was horrific. So, I'd be sitting in the back room, off where the guys were cutting meat up, and I'm putting potatoes in brown paper bags.

One of the boys would always open the curtain to ask me if I was eating any of that candy that was sitting around back there, I said, "No, I'm not eating any of it. I'm trying to learn my lesson."

Finally, he said, "You know, I think you ought to be whistling while you're working back here and that way we'll know that you're not stuffing your mouth full of candy."

I said, "Okay." So, I sat there and whistled and worked, and every once in a while he'd open the curtain and have a little tiny ball of hamburger and pitch that at me and hit me on the head a few times. That was all done in fun and games, I know. I probably had that job for a week to pay off the candy.

Cleaning Bricks at the Old School

My brother came home one day, I think I was about 7, and he asked me if I wanted to help clean bricks down at the old school where they'd pretty much knocked most of the old school down. There were piles of brick everywhere, and I said, "Sure, what's it pay?" "Well, they'll pay ya a penny a brick to knock all the old mortar off the bricks and put them up in stacks." That sounded like a good deal to me. We went down there, knocked the mortar off the old bricks and put them in stacks.

They had a crew that had come up from Concordia that was kind of a family operation. The old man, he was a little on the crazy side.

One time, one of my brother's buddies said to me, "Why don't you go over there and work on that pile over there. That's a real nice pile of bricks over there."

So, I took my hammer and I went over there and started cleaning. I was like the canary in the coal mine. All of a sudden I looked up. The foreman from the Concordia crew was standing over me with a hammer in his hand.

He said, "You little SOB, you best get the hell out of here now."

I went scrambling over to where my brother was working. The old man would walk around with sticks of dynamite in his back pocket. Every once in a while he would put a stick of dynamite on a wall and he'd light a fuse and BOOM, there was a rock slide everywhere. I guess that was part of the deal. After the first week I got a payment of $2.00 and some odd cents. When you're about 7 years old that was big money.

Outsmarting a Politician

I'll never forget when I was about 7 years old, my little buddy and I were riding bicycles on a hot July day. It was so hot and humid, it was unbearable. We sat down on the curb, trying to put the chain back on my bicycle, looked across the street to my neighbor's house, and a big, old, black, probably Lincoln car, had stopped and this man started walking across the street. I remember he had a black suit on, and a white tie. I thought, what a day for a black suit, it's got to be so hot. He came over to introduce himself.

He said, "My name is Bob Dole, and I'm running for a political office here in Kansas. I was wondering if you boys would like to have some fun today."

I said, "What do you got in mind?"

"Well, I've got this box of bumper stickers I need to get put on the bumpers of all these cars in this town."

I said, "Well, what if I put a bumper sticker on somebody's car that wants to vote for the other man?"

He looked and said, "Well, that's not a problem. He can peel that bumper sticker off then."

I thought, "Yeah right."

The bumpers were chrome plated, and once you put one of those bumper stickers on it, it stays there until that car goes to the junk yard. You can't tear them off. I thought, well this guy's not very honest, but I told him, "Yeah, I think we can do that for you, Mr. Dole."

He said, "Okay." He sat down the box of bumper stickers and I thought maybe he'd flip us a quarter for our time. He just walked away. So I thought, well, two can play this kind of game.

So I hollered at him, I said, "Hey, Mr. Dole, I don't think one box of bumper stickers will be enough because there's lot of farmers who live around here and come into town."

He said, "Oh, okay, I'll get you another one then." He popped open the trunk of his car and got another box out and brought it over. Then he took off.

So my little buddy, his name was Dana Elnif, he looked at me and said, "Jim, what are we going to do with all these bumper stickers?"

I said, "I don't know what we're going to do with them, but I know what we're not going to do with them. We're not going to go around and put them on people's bumpers." The more that I looked at the bumper stickers, I realized that my buddy's name started with a "D" and his last name started with an "E", so I looked at that word Dole and I said "I know what we're going to do with them. I'm going to borrow a pair of scissors from mom and we'll cut out all the Ds and Es out of the word Dole. Those are your initials and we can put those on your bicycle." So that's what we did. We cut out all the Ds and Es, plastered his bicycle with his initials, and then ended up throwing the rest of those stickers in the trash.

James Grennan

Watermelon along the River

When I was a kid I was always jumping in the old '51 Ford with my mom. We'd go down to the grocery store, come home, or maybe we'd run to Concordia. Certain time of the year there was a sweet old guy along the river, who raised watermelon. I'd always try to get mom to pull down there and buy a watermelon or two. She usually would and we'd go down there and water-melons were like a penny a pound. After we paid the old man, he used to always insist that we take an extra watermelon home with us. That made those watermelons a half-a-penny a pound. They were big watermelon too, at least 20-30 pounds. Boy, were they good.

"Farming looks mighty easy when your plow is a pencil and you're a thousand miles from the corn field." Dwight D. Eisenhower

BB Gun Battles Down At the Jungle

We used to have a field a quarter of a mile southeast of the house, and over the years, volunteer trees over took it. It was probably about an acre of ground, and we kids, we called it the "jungle." We'd go down there with our BB guns and we'd have what we called BB gun battles.

While we were down there, we'd take old sunflower stalks, take our pocket knives, whittle them down and make spears out of them. We'd chase each other around in the jungle, shoot each other with BB guns, and throw spears at each other. I remember one time I caught a spear in the middle of my back running away from an older kid. Boy did that hurt, but I guess it didn't hurt me enough to send me to the hospital.

Everything was all fine and dandy until my second oldest brother shot my oldest brother in the eye with a BB. When my dad came home he was one unhappy camper. He had to take him to the hospital to get his eye patched up.

I remember walking into the downstairs bathroom and seeing that BB gun busted in half in the waste basket. I was distraught! I fished it out and took it over to my mother. She was washing dishes. I was crying about it and she said, "Oh, don't worry about it Jim, we'll take it down to that old man that I do washing for on Saturdays, and I bet he can fix it and put a new stock on it." Sure enough, that old man made it look like a brand new BB gun. I don't think my dad ever knew about it. I think we put it away somewhere where he wouldn't even know we had it fixed.

One time while we were leaving the jungle, one of the boys had a pellet gun. We decided to pump it up until it wouldn't pump anymore and see how far it would drive a pellet into a fence post. We must have pumped it a hundred times. Only problem was he forgot to load it with the pellet.

Fishing In the Rain under the Bridge

When I was in the second or third grade, I wanted to go fishing and catch a big old catfish. I had been thinking about this when in the Weekly Reader, I think it was called, there was this boy who went out and caught a catfish. Oh, did that look good!

I started asking around and some of the old guys around town who went fishing a lot, they told me the best time to catch a fish is when it's raining. "Really?" "Yeah!" So, one Saturday morning I woke up and it was raining. I grabbed my fishing pole and walked in the rain about a half mile to the creek, went down in there and threw my bait in the water. It kept raining. The rain kept getting worse and worse, and I thought, I'm not leaving until I catch a fish.

After a couple of hours, I went back home. I never even got a bite! I never have figured out if that was a "truism" or just a big lie. I guess I probably will never know now.

Later, I went fishing and caught a nice sized Carp. I was told that Carp weren't good to eat. I gave it to my mother and she cut the mud vein out of it and baked it in the oven with some potatoes and onions. It was the best fish meal I can ever remember eating.

Kansas City Scales Out of Whack

I'll never forget when I was 7 or 8 years old, my dad took his truck and trailer that he went to Kansas City with, and started going all over the Midwest, hauling corn and milo. He'd go to North and South Dakota in the winter time.

He came home one cold winter day and I was watching him as he was coming up the sidewalk. He had a whole arm full of gunny sacks and flopped them on the living room floor.

I said, "Dad, what are all these gunny sacks about?"

He said, "Come in the kitchen, sit down and I'll tell you what's going on." I went into the kitchen, sat down and he says, "Jim, here lately on loads to Kansas City, I've been coming up about 200 to 225 pounds short. What I want you to do is go out there with these gunny sacks, take your hammer and nails, and nail these gunny sacks to the trailer floor. If that thing is leaking any wheat, it will be coming from the floor of the trailer."

So, I said okay and went out there, crawled up on the back of the trailer, undid the tarp and threw it up far enough so I could get a little light in there. Oh, man, was it cold, it was so bitter cold. It was just unbelievably cold, but I had a job to do so I did it.

Dad went back the next day, loaded up the wheat and took off for Kansas City. That night, I watched for him. About 6 o'clock, he came home, got out of his truck, and he had another load of gunny sacks in his arms.

He came in, threw them down and he said, "They claim I was 220 lbs short." So he had me take those gunny sacks and nail them up on the sides of that trailer. It was colder than blazes, but I managed to get it done. He did the same thing the next day. He went down, loaded up, and took another load to Kansas City. That night, I watched for him. 6 o'clock, no dad. 7 o'clock, he still isn't home. 8 o'clock..., finally about 9 o'clock I saw the lights of his truck coming down the road.

He came in, and I asked, "Did you lose any wheat?"

Dad's pup and trailer

He said, "Come in and sit down in the kitchen and I'll tell you what happened." So, I went into the kitchen and he said, "When I got unloaded, they handed me my ticket, 220 lbs short! So, I told the guys that I was going to go across the street to the cafeteria and have me a bite to eat and call the scale boys and have these here scales checked out!" He said the guy told him, that he couldn't just leave his truck and trailer on the scales, and my dad said "You just hide and watch."

So he walked over to the cafeteria and called the scale boys. There were probably about 50 semis in line behind him and they were hollering and madder than hell at him, because he basically shut the elevator down. The scale boys came and sure enough, the scales were about 220 lbs off. Days later, every grain hauler that would see him coming up Highway 24, they'd flash their lights, roll down their windows and wave at him. He said it was all worth it in the end to get those scales fixed where they weren't cheating everybody out of about 220 lbs. I was really impressed with my dad's tenacity to stand up for what was right.

My Doodle Bug Mechanic

My dad was a WWII veteran. When he came back from the war, he wasn't the same person that they sent over there. Our little town was chuck full of WWII vets, and too many of them just couldn't take it, couldn't handle it, and they would end up committing suicide. Probably at least half of the ones that I knew decided to check out early. It was a very sad situation. They were very sweet and kind people, but they had major mental issues.

I remember when I was 7 or 8 I had a little motorized bike that I called my "doodle bug." There was this old guy by the name of Alfe Metro, who was a WWII vet that was so shell shocked he could hardly talk. But every time I rode on my doodle bug and it needed a little tensioning, I'd go over and he'd pull up a little stool and work on it until he got it going again. I'll never forget him, that's for sure.

Dad's Wisdom and Memorable Sayings

John Grennan in semi

Some of the things my dad told me, when I was a kid I have never forgotten. I'd always badgered him to take me with him on the semi. He did, and one time we had to relieve ourselves along the road. We were back there relieving ourselves, and I told dad, "Dad there are cars coming toward us." He said, "They know what we're doing but they can't see us, so it doesn't matter!" Some real truth to that I thought.

Dad used to like to say, "You can call me any derogatory word you can think of as long as you say it in a nice tone of voice."

I remember my dad saying that if he taught us kids to say please, thank you, and you're welcome, he considered his life a success.

One other time, dad was at home sleeping after a trip in the semi. I went in and woke him up and I said, "Dad, you're always driving that truck and it doesn't seem like you're ever really making any money. How can a person make money other than doing this?" He kind of set up in the bed and he said, "Jim, if you want to make money, go get yourself some cows. At night they're out there eating hay or grass while you're sleeping, they're making you money. That truck out there, when I'm sleeping, it's costing me money. That's money I got to make up somehow. The insurance never stops, tags, all that stuff, it's going on whether you're sleeping or driving it." I thought that was pretty good thing to remember.

One other time, he took me down to the Vet's Club and I remember walking up the stairs and went in, and there were four or five old farmers sitting there playing poker and he politely said, "Would you mind if I joined you?" They all kind of looked up, well, they couldn't say no, because he literally had a reputation of being the best poker player in Kansas. I'd be 200 miles from home, tell them what my name was and they'd say, "Oh, are you related to John Grennan?" I would say, "Yes," and they would say, "Well, you know he's the best poker player in Kansas." So he had quite a reputation of being a good poker player. So, that day at the Vet's Club, he sat down with those folks, played some poker, won a few bucks, and then he politely excused himself. Of course, that didn't make anybody happy when he got up and left the poker game with some of their money, but that's just the way it was. Only problem was he loved to take his poker winnings and head over to the crap table. He always told me that playing poker was just too slow and boring.

One Saturday morning I walked out into the kitchen. Dad was sitting at the kitchen table, head down, and I said, "Dad, what's wrong?" He said, "Well Jim, I was rolling the dice last night, one time I was $3,800 ahead. Then the dice went cold. I lost all that plus some of my money." I said, "Dad, why didn't you quit when you were $3,800 ahead?" He looked at me and said, "Well, Jim, if I had known that, why didn't I quit when I was $1,800 ahead?" I'll never forget that, there's some truth to that.

27

Early 4th of July

My dad was a survivor of World War II, being one of the guys that were able to make it home. My uncle said my dad never touched a drop until he went into the Service, and when he came out he was a full-fledged alcoholic.

He'd always have a half pint of Sunny Brook tucked down in his boot. One time I asked him how come those Sunny Brook bottles had that curve in them.

He said, "Well, it's real simple. You put it down your boot. It's curved to your leg and nobody will ever know you have it."

In the spring of the year, after all the cold winter months there in Kansas, we'd take the trash out and put it in a big pile out there in the back yard. We'd light a match to it and burn down all that trash. I remember sneaking out there more than once, finding some of his old half pint Sunny Brook bottles. I'd unscrew the cap and have me a few drinks of what came out of the bottom of the bottle. I don't ever remember getting too jacked up, but I'm sure I did. When we burned down that pile of trash, it was like an early 4th of July for us kids because a couple hundred Sunny Brook bottles were exploding big time.

Sunday Night TV at the Neighbor's

In the '50s, the black and white TV emerged upon the scene. We were always trying to talk our folks into buying us a TV. My dad said we were never going to have a TV in our house because there was nothing but trash coming from it. He finally agreed to let us go on Sunday nights to a couple of our neighbors houses to watch it with them. We watched The Lawrence Welk Show and Bonanza on Sunday nights. We thought that was a real treat to be able to go watch TV at the neighbor's on Sunday nights!

I used to have an uncle that was slick bald. When he came to visit he always accused my younger brother and me of polishing apples for our teachers. He let me rub his slick head and I would ask him how he was able to get his head so bald. I thought being bald looked so cool. He said, "Jim, if you want to become bald like me, wear a hat all the time and never take it off." So I thought, well, if that's what it takes, that's what I'll have to do.

One night, my brother and I were walking over to the neighbor's to watch TV. Of course I had my hat on. My brother stopped us under the street light. He said to me, "Jim, take that stupid looking hat off or we are not going over to watch TV tonight." I tried to explain to him I had to always wear it or I wouldn't go bald like my Uncle Albert. I couldn't sway him around to my way of thinking so I had to take my hat off.

So, we got over to the old farmer's house and as we were watching TV, he and his wife were eating their T-bone steaks in the kitchen. The aroma was driving us crazy! When Bonanza was over and we were getting ready to head home, he asked us if we would like to take a bag of meat home with us. Of course we would, I told him. My dad and him never really liked each other too much, and when we got that bag home and opened it on our kitchen table, there was nothing but big old cow bones in that sack. They didn't have any meat on them. We gave those bones to our dog to chew on.

Old Charlie Beating the System

I'd go downtown with my mom and every time we'd see old Charlie, an old man living in a little shack there in town. He was always walking to his house or walking toward town to the grocery store.

Finally, I asked my mom, "How come that guy is always walking to the grocery store? Why doesn't he pick up what he needs in one trip? That way he wouldn't have to make so many trips."

She said, "Well, because if you buy something at the grocery store that's 29 cents or less, there's no tax on it. Everything over 29 cents they start putting a penny sales tax on it. He figures he could save that penny by making three or four trips instead of getting all his groceries in one shot."

I thought that was pretty clever of the old man. He was able to beat the system in his own little way.

Dad's Drunken Helpers

My dad, he'd always hire these less than scrupulous people out there in the world. One guy that he hired was named Ray. Ray's girlfriend was Dorothy. They were just total alcoholics. They couldn't drink enough, fast enough, long enough.

One night, they came up to our house. They had a whole bushel basket of grapes. They were drunker than skunks. When they got there, of course, they just kind of came in, took over my mom's kitchen. They asked my mom if they could smash grapes with their feet in her kitchen. Of course, she was like, you have got to be kidding me. But what could she say? They proceeded to smash those grapes with their feet there in mom's kitchen. They were just dead drunk anyway, and walking around smashing grapes and messing up mom's kitchen. I thought to myself, "Mom, can't you tell these people just to get out of your kitchen and go?" But, she wasn't that type of person, and she put up with it. Always wondered how she dealt with some of that craziness, but she did.

Dad hired Ray to drive his semi a few times. I remember the time he called from western Kansas to tell my dad that he had tipped the semi over in the ditch. Dad was able to go out and retrieve his wrecked semi. I remember my two older brothers having to rebuild the broken side boards. I can't remember how dad got that semi righted. But I did see a picture of the semi laid on its side in the ditch.

Hay hauler

Second Grade Accident

I'll never forget one warm fall day, in second grade. We're all sitting there in school, very quiet. The classes had pretty much just started, and uh, I had an accident. It was just a terrific smelling situation all around me and of course, it drifted up to the teacher.

When she realized what had happened, she very sweetly and politely just said, "Well, if somebody needs to go the bathroom, just get up and go. You know it's not that big a deal."

I was sitting there and thinking to myself, well, if I get up and go, then everybody in this class is going to know who did this. If I sit here until class is over, and walk out with everybody, then maybe nobody would know it was me. So, I sat there.

Of course, it ended up with the smell getting worse and worse, and the teacher, poor teacher, she went over and opened up a couple of windows. A few minutes later, she went over and opened up all of the windows. The whole class was in agony, but I was certainly not going to get up at that stage and walk out of there because everybody would be pointing to me. I thought I'd rather take my chances. So I sat there thinking to myself, this class will be over sooner or later, and sure enough it was. I got up with the class, proceeded to walk out. To this day I don't know how many people realized it was me that had the accident.

Hunting Rabbits with My Brother

I remember the time, I was probably 8 years old and my middle brother was 12, we were up in the boys' bedroom and he came walking out of the closet with something wrapped up in a pillowcase.

I asked him, "What have you got there?"

He said, "I'll show it to you if you promise not to tell Mom or Dad."

"Okay, I won't tell anybody."

He pulled out a 2 1/2 foot long, single shot, bolt action 22 rifle. I thought, wow, that's pretty cool!

I took the bolt out of it and looked down the barrel, I couldn't see any light. I asked my brother, "Shouldn't you be able to see light down this barrel?"

He said, "Well, yeah!"

"Well, you can't," I said.

He looked and he couldn't see light either. So, he said, "It's got a crooked barrel." He went over and stuck the barrel in the old steam radiator, gave it a jerk, pulled it back out. I looked at it and it looked straight as an arrow. "Well, I guess that fixed it," he said.

We then took off and went down to the creek, rabbit hunting and there was a rabbit sitting over on the side of the bank and he aimed at it, "bang," there goes the rabbit. So I went over and picked up the rabbit. We walked down the creek a ways and there's another rabbit. He put his gun on it, "bang." So now we've got two rabbits. I'm thinking to myself that this doesn't seem too fair. Ought to at least give the rabbit a sporting chance.

So I told him, "How 'bout if I take a snowball, next rabbit we see, I'll throw a snowball at it, at least it will be running and it will have a chance."

My brother said "Okay, we can do that." So the next rabbit we saw, I threw a snowball at it, and it went hopping off down the side of the creek bed. While it's running, he aims and "bang." Now we've got three rabbits. I look back at my brother and think he's quite the marksman.

Well, he went to the Army. He won several shooting awards, so he was definitely a marksman. A little 2-1/2 foot rifle that had a crooked barrel and he could still get rabbits on the run. I was totally amazed. It started making sense to me why the guy that sold that unsafe rifle to my 12-yr old brother had such a bad name around the town.

Farming First Year

The year I turned 10 years old, my dad came up to me in the spring and he said, "Do you think you're old enough to run a tractor this summer?"

I said, "Well, of course."

So he said, "Okay." He decided to trade the old "D" off for a John Deere 70 Diesel. We jumped in the car and went down to Concordia and dad asked if I could drive the John Deere home. I thought, well, of course I can.

When I got up on that tractor, he got up there with me and said, "Here's your clutch [it had an old hand clutch], there's the brakes, in case you need them, here's where you put it in gear, and here's your throttle."

So I took off. Pretty soon I saw him, he had his hand out the window of the car trying to flag me down, and I grabbed the hand clutch, only problem was I didn't have enough strength to snap it out of gear. He realized I was in trouble and he pulled up alongside me. "What's the matter?" he asked.

"I can't pull the clutch back to stop it," I said.

He told me to idle it clear down and stomp on the brakes and try to kill it. So I did. I got the tractor stopped.

Dad got under there and loosened the mechanism on the clutch so it wouldn't be so hard to snap back out of gear, and away we went. We both got home. The first day we took the tractor and hooked it onto the plow. After the wheat was cut, I asked him, "How much are you going to pay me?"

"I think I can pay you about 50 cents an hour," he said.

I thought that was pretty good money. So, he said to me, "Keep track of your hours, and at the end of the summer, we'll settle up." I said, "Okay."

I ran that tractor all summer long, had somewhere around 800 hours, if I remember right. The best I can remember is he owed me about $400.00. So I said, "Well, Dad, I need my money now."

Jim's first year farming
L-R: Kevin, Jim, Cousin Jimmy

He said, "I don't know how to tell you this Jim, but I just don't have $400.00." I thought, well, looks like I might have worked all summer for nothing.

So, I went upstairs, drew me a hot bath and I was sitting in the bathtub thinking about working all summer for nothing. He heard me crying, I suppose. He came up and knocked on the door. I told him to come in. He said, "Jim, I don't know how to tell you how sorry I am, but we just had an unprofitable summer." He reached in his billfold and pulls out a $50 bill. He sat it on the sink and said, "At least I can pay you this." And I looked at that $50 bill and I thought, you know, he feels worse about this than I do. He's put a roof over my head, fed me all summer, so how could I not feel anything but good.

James Grennan

What Are You Sitting There For?

One other time I was plowing the wheat stubble down where the stubble was a lot thicker and I was having a little trouble getting through it with the plow, which was plugging up. So I pulled up to dad as he was lighting the wheat stubble on fire down in the draw. That was the way we did it, so we wouldn't have to worry about plugging up the plow. He had a pretty good fire going across the draw. I sat there, and he came up and said, "What are you sitting here for?"

I said, "With that fire, I'm not going to drive this tractor through that."

He said, "You need to just keep going, because this is a diesel tractor and you're not going to have to worry about it blowing up."

I proceeded to plow on down through the fire in several places. I hoped that sucker doesn't blow up on me while I'm going through there, and it didn't.

"Whether it's on the tractor or in the pasture with the cows, I just love being able to take my kids to work when I need to." Will Collier

My Finger Smashing Ordeal

One time my dad came up to me and told me he had purchased a harrow and we needed to go out to the carter quarter, unhook the plow and hook up the harrow and try it out. After we hooked it up, I sat on the fender so he could drive the tractor to test it out. Only problem was the hitch was too short, so when he made the first turn, the harrow rode up the tire and smashed my finger between it and the fender. It really did a number on my finger. The pain seemed to go away when he got tears in his eyes and kept telling me over and over how sorry he was for smashing my finger. It is no wonder farming is such a high risk occupation.

"The farmer has to be an optimist or he wouldn't still be a farmer." Will Rogers

Keeping Me Out of Trouble

It always seemed my dad tried to make us boys as tough as he could. His real goal or aim was to try to keep us out of town. He'd keep us on the tractors. One time, I'd been working for many days straight, disking the weeds down in every field where we had been harvesting. When we got all caught up, I was one happy camper because I thought I could take a couple of days off.

Ace and Del finding some shade

So I went up to my dad, and said something like "Dad, looks like we're pretty well caught up. We've got all the field work done." I figured he'd say to take the tractor and just park it and take a couple of days off. Nope.

He said, "You know you've been working in that field north to south. Now what I want you to do is start working that field east to west."

I thought to myself, you've got to be kidding me! Anything to keep me in the field and out of town.

Tractor Power Solution

I was running my dad's tractor, plowing ground a couple of miles west of town. The old tractor was getting where it was losing a little power. When I told my dad, I said, "Dad, you know I can't really farm in third gear anymore. The tractor is losing a little power, and now I have to shift and put it into second gear."

He said, "Well, I'll tell you what I'll do. I'm going to go down to the John Deere dealer and see if I can't figure out something." So he did, and he came back and said, "Jim, I traded that 4 bottom 4/14 plow in for a 3 bottom 3/16 plow, so instead of covering like 56 inches, we'll be covering like 48 inches, but I think you can now plow in third gear."

So that's what he did, that's how he solved that problem. I'll never forget that, I thought that was pretty strange, but that's what happened. He sure didn't have the money to trade for a little better tractor.

Farming My Own Wheat Field

When I was about 11, I decided to try my own hand at farming on my one acre patch of ground just a little ways from our house on the edge of town with the 70 D tractor. We didn't have a fuel wagon, so my dad stuck a couple of barrel tanks on the side of the tractor to keep fuel in so we could stay out in the field a lot longer before we had to come to town and fuel up. The tractor had a little tiny 4-cylinder "starting motor" on it to turn the tractor over to start the main engine. I'd grab an empty oil can and I'd go down to the Coop, put about five cents worth of gas in that oil can for starting the motor and the guy at the Coop would say, "You're costing me more to process this paperwork than that 5 cents worth of gas your buying." You know, he was just kidding me, but I'll never forget him talking to me about that.

Every time I'd come into town with the Tandem disk, I'd run that disk over the one acre field of wheat that I was getting ready to plant in the fall and this field had a lot of bindweed in it. So every time I'd disk it, it would put down more bindweed sprouts. In June, a couple of my brothers would go cut the wheat, and all that bindweed would wind around the wheat heads and pretty much choke them out, but we'd cut it anyway. We took out about 14 bushels, which was about half bindweed seeds and half wheat.

We took it down to the elevator and the old boy that ran the elevator said, "We'll need to probe it." So, he went out and looked over the side of the truck bed and said that this wasn't wheat, it was mostly bindweed! He told me, "I don't even know if I can take it or accept it." He went in and came back out and said that this would be a one-time deal. He was going to go ahead and take it, but thought maybe he could mix it with some dry wheat, so that's what he did.

The funny part of it was that for two or three years, I'd see him on Main Street in Jamestown, maybe across the street, and he'd just burst out laughing. He had a real deep laugh and everybody in town could hear him. He'd holler across the street at me, he says "Jim, you got any more bindweed seed you'd like to sell?" Then he'd start laughing. It was kind of funny, I thought. No wonder people around me called me a stubble bum.

Brother Pat heading to my 1 acre field

The Scariest Ride of My Life

When I was 12 and my brother was 16, he finished up the wheat harvest in northern Montana. He was able to hitch a ride with my uncle's combining partner as far south as Oberlin, Kansas, who was going on south to his house in southwest Oklahoma. My brother called his best buddy and asked him if he could come out and pick him up. "Of course," he said. My brother asked him to stop by our house in Jamestown and pick me up because my brother wanted to see me. The friend really wasn't thrilled to have me tagging along, so he told me I would have to ride in the back seat. I crawled back there.

The seats were made of leather in his '57 Ford, hopped up convertible with the top down. Being leather seats, they were slicker than snot. Nothing to hang on to, and away we went. Between Jamestown and Randall there is a set of hills that remind you of a rollercoaster ride. I was terrified that I was going to fly out the back of that car! Why I didn't, to this day I'll never know. I remember that it was about 155 miles from Jamestown to Oberlin, which took us all of 90 minutes to make that drive, averaging over 100 mph. Wow, what a scary trip that turned out to be!

Two Crashes for the Price of One

There was an old WWII veteran that lived three or four houses down from our house to the south of us. He, like so many of those poor guys, had a very bad drinking problem.

One late night when I was sound asleep, I was awakened by the sound of a loud crash outside at the corner of our house. I woke up, looked out the window, and this guy had turned the corner too sharp and smashed his old pickup truck into the fire hydrant. When I looked out there, he was just sitting in his pickup with his lights on and steam coming out of the radiator of his smashed-in pickup. Why it didn't break the fire hydrant off, I'll never know. I watched to see what might happen next. He must have sat there for a good 5 minutes.

All of a sudden, he put the truck in reverse and backed up, probably a good 10 to 15 feet. He stopped, put it back in low gear, and plowed ahead until he smashed into the fire hydrant a second time. I watched for a few more minutes, and then I went back to bed. The next morning his pickup was gone, so I assumed he was able to drive it down the block. He definitely had at least one drink too many that night!

Raising Pet Pigs in Town

When I was about 12, my best buddy lived on a farm and his dad raised cattle and hogs. We talked about me trying my hand at raising some hogs myself there in town. That was a total no-no, but people were, well, a little bit more understanding back then. I took the old chicken coup, fixed it up the best I could, bought a couple of little tiny wiener pigs from that guy for $5 apiece.

I would go out of town and gather up some corn lying in the corn fields that didn't get run through the combine. We'd take gunny sacks and fill them up. My brother and sister helped me and I would also get food scraps from school. The school had lots of leftover food scraps from the lunches that kids didn't eat, so I'd bring them home and feed that to the pigs. Those pigs got up to about 210 pounds. They had, by that time, become pet pigs. They would get up on their hind legs on the fence when they would see me coming home from school.

Then I found out that those pigs had what they called back then "crooked nose disease." Their snouts were turned and it made it really hard for them to breathe. I didn't know at the time but it was a very contagious disease. But came the day I had to sell them to the slaughter house, my buddy's dad brought his pickup in and helped me load those pigs up.

He said, "Jim, you know, I don't know if we're going to be able to sell these pigs. That's a pretty contagious disease that those hogs have." I said, "Well, we gotta do what we gotta do."

We went to the sale barn. My buddy's dad told me to wait in the pickup, and said he was going to go in and talk to the guy and see what he could work out with him. So I sat in the pickup. It seemed like half an hour, but pretty soon, he came back out and told me the sale barn was going to take those pigs just this one time. He sure didn't want to, but he said he would. So, we got them out, weighed them, and he wrote me a check for $33.00 for those two 220-lb hogs. I was able to get rid of them and that was the end of my hog raising adventure.

Jim and his two pet pigs

Very Kind People

When we were growing up, my dad, with his seven kids, things weren't too profitable, so to speak, so we were able to actually charge our groceries at the grocery store. Then in the summer when we cut the wheat, he'd go down and pay our grocery bill off. We were very fortunate to know folks like Don Hutchinson who owned the grocery store. My dad was also able to borrow money at the Glasco bank (about 30 miles from Jamestown). I can't remember the names of the people that ran that bank, but they were very nice people. They were very understanding, and they'd loan my dad a little money once in a while when they knew he didn't have any collateral. Things were a little different back in those days.

"My grandfather used to say that once in your life you need a doctor, a lawyer, a policeman, and a preacher. But every day, three times a day, you need a farmer."
Brenda Schoepp

Relaxing Under the Bridge

One hot summer day, when I was 12 or 13 maybe, my buddy would come along and say, "Hey Jim, let's go out, take a hike. Let's go down to the creek and get under the bridge where it's cool." I said, "Okay, that's sounds like fun to me." Along we went. After we got out of town a little bit, he said, "I got a pack of cigarettes." I thought, well, that's okay.

We were walking along the ditch and found a six-pack of beer that somebody probably threw out for whatever reason. Five beers were still left in that six pack, so we picked that up. We got to the bridge and sat there under the bridge, smoking cigarettes and drank those hot beers and had a good old time, talking about the hot girls and women in the town. Looking back, it all makes sense that my dad always wanted me on a tractor. He knew how easy it was for young boys to get into trouble.

Illegal Carp Fishing with Cherry Bombs

I had a buddy whose dad drove semis. When he was down south, driving his truck, he would bring back what they called "cherry bombs" and "silver salutes"; very, very powerful firecrackers, I guess you'd call them. So, one day we thought we'd take a box of these firecrackers out to what they called the Jamestown State Lake. It was kind of a marshy area, where the water sits for several acres.

That lake had a lot of carp in it. It was only about a foot deep, so we started wading in there, chasing the carp, and started throwing those cherry bombs at them. We must have gone through almost a whole box of cherry bombs and never got one fish. Somebody asked me later why I didn't tie a rock or something heavy to those cherry bombs, then they'd sink and I probably would have had some fish. I thought that made a lot of sense.

Later, after hearing this, we went to the creek and tried this idea, but had no luck. Probably would have worked had there been fish in that creek. We should have gone back out to the lake.

14-Year Old Harvest Boy

When I turned 14 my dad asked me, "Jim, do you think you're old enough now to run a combine all summer on the harvest run?"

I said, "Well, of course."

My dad then told me he had just traded off the '55 John Deere highboy for a Carryover 1963 Lowboy with a 14-foot header on it, which would be what I would run. My brother, he was four years older than I was, he'd been on the harvest for two or three years, and he was going to be my mentor.

We were headed for Oklahoma, down on the Red River between Oklahoma and Texas, around the Temple, Oklahoma area. We went down in the old farm truck, a 1948 Ford that was named Big Red, and he was driving and he was trying to tell me the do's and don'ts and what to expect. I'm riding shot gun with my new white cowboy hat and new boots.

Trying to mentor me on the way, and about every two hours, he'd say, "Now Jim, you got to remember you got that auger sticking out there. If you have a brain fart for one second, a telephone pole or something will jump out and tear that auger off."

I said, "Okay, Pat, okay. I'll remember that."

Again, about every two hours he'd tell me that same thing again. "When we get down to Oklahoma with that brand new machine, the first round around the field you need to go back-ward so the auger is pointing into the field, not out where if there's any telephone poles along the edges of the fields, you don't have to worry about them."

So, I made that first round and he jumps up on the combine and said, "How's everything?" Yeah, everything's fine, oil temperature, yeah, water, yeah, and starts back down the ladder of the combine, he turns around and he says, "Just remember one thing. Don't forget that auger sticking out there."

I said, "Okay", and I thought, what does he think I am, a complete idiot? He's constantly reminding me about this auger situation. He

51

reminded me all the way down here, we came to this little field, all across the "tullies" (Kansas slang for sticks) to the next wheat field.

Jim cutting the carter quarter

We approached this old homestead that had been there probably when the Oklahoma land rush was going on, I started going through that barnyard. All of a sudden, I looked over to my left and there's a light pole. Well, might as well say it, it was too late. My auger hit that light pole, and swung it out. That pole had been in the ground so long, it was so rotted at its bottom, so it didn't bust my auger off, but my auger busted that light pole off. There was a big old squish in the auger, but it didn't tear it off. Well, I thought, I've dodged the bullet this time. I pulled up and unloaded some wheat.

My brother looked at the squish in the auger and he said, "I'm not even going to ask you what happened."

I said, "Well, you were right. That light pole jumped out and got me." He never said another word about it ever again, and needless to say, I never made that mistake again.

Watching for Snakes along the Red River

We were working along the Red River and it was getting about dark. The farmer we were cutting for came up and told me this was rattlesnake country, and if something would happen to my combine, don't get off, just don't get off your combine, because there are rattlesnakes everywhere. I thought to myself, I don't want to hear that. I started cutting that little field, and pretty soon it's dark and I thought to myself, I wonder if he's telling me the real truth about the rattlesnakes down here. I just shut off my combine and started to listen to see if I could hear those rattlesnakes. There were rattles, everywhere, and I thought, "Oh, my goodness! Somehow get me out of here alive." Eventually, I needed to get back to the pickup, so I tiptoed very gently through the field. At least I had my cowboy boots on to help against a snake strike. I was terrified!

53

Not My First Beer

I remember the time we had just finished cutting wheat in the Temple, Oklahoma area. It was probably 7-8 o'clock at night. We pulled into town and had something to eat. The older guys said, "Let's go over here and have a cold beer, and yeah, Jim, you can come along. You're only 14 and you can't have a beer, but you can sure get a soda pop." So, I said, "That'll work."

We went into the bar and everybody ordered their beers. I was sitting on the end of the bar there and the guy running the bar asked, "What can I get for you?"

I said, "Well, I'd really like to have a cold beer, but I'm only 14, so I'm sure that's out of the question."

He says, "Well, son, you've been out in the harvest field working just like a grown man. So, what kind of beer do you want?"

"Well, give me a Schlitz then." This is a memory that makes me smile. I certainly felt like I deserved that beer.

Jim's '63 Combine

"Agriculture is our wisest pursuit, because it will in the end contribute most to real wealth, good morals and happiness." Thomas Jefferson

Kennedy Halves at the Carnival

The first year on the harvest was 1964 for me, and that was the year that they made the last of the 90% silver Kennedy half dollars. Every time I'd go into a restaurant to pay for my meal, if I got a 50-cent piece, I'd save it. I saved Kennedy halves all summer long. Finally made it up to Glendive, Montana and one day, it rained.

I found a cute little carnival girl, and I thought I was in love with her. That was the centennial year for Montana becoming a territory. Her family and a bunch of other folks had a carnival set up on the main street of Glendive. One night at the carnival, I had 80 to 100 Kennedy halves and I was bound and determined I was going to win this little gal a teddy bear. I remember the game was to pitch a ball in a peach basket with a hole cut out in the bottom of it. If you could throw a ball without it bouncing out, you could win a prize. Win enough prizes you could change them in for a teddy bear. So I started playing. Of course, every time I threw a ball the thing would bounce out.

Finally the guy comes around and he said, "You're just too nervous or some-thing. I'll show you just how easy this is." He threw a ball and it went right down the hole.

I thought, "Well, I guess maybe I am doing something wrong." After all was said and done, I went through probably 80 Kennedy halves. Never once did that ball fall down through that hole. After saving up all those Kennedy halves just to see them all go bye-bye.

Pool, Pinball, and Cheap Beer

When I turned about 15 years old, there wasn't much to do in our little town except to work, drink, or chase girls. I seemed to excel in the first two - not so good in the third one. The local pool hall became my second home.

The 80-year old man that ran our pool hall didn't much care how old you were as long as you had money to pay for your beers. I asked him one time why he never drank beer with us and he told me that beer was made for selling, not for drinking. I remember the time he raised the price of a glass of beer from 10 cents a glass to 20 cents a glass in one day. We were fit to be tied until he told us his keg prices went up and the glasses went from 7 ounces to 11 ounces.

We had a snooker table instead of a pool table to practice on. This made me a very good pool player because of the pocket size difference.

There was a pinball machine that we use to put match books under the front legs so it would give us a lot of free games. The old guy figured out how we were always winning free games, so one time he came over and unplugged the machine and told us our pinball days were over.

Young Lust

When I was on the harvest crew down in southern Oklahoma, I ran into this little 14-year old girl. I was 16. She wanted to be boyfriend/girlfriend. One day when it rained, I asked my uncle if I could go over and visit with her. She wanted me to come over to her house. Play "tiddlywinks" I thought, probably. My uncle said it would be all right, so I walk over and knocked on her door. She came to the door in a muumuu. She was 14 years old and totally developed. So, I went in, and sure enough, she told me to come on back to the bedroom. I'd always heard that southern girls were a lot more mature at a young age.

Chewing for $5.00

When I was 15, my second year on the harvest run, we were in Jamestown. I was getting ready to load my combine onto my Ford truck. One of the guys my uncle hired from southeastern Kansas came up and he had a can of Shoal chewing tobacco.

He said, "Jim, if you can chew this tobacco for a week, and if you do, I'll give you $5.00."

I said that I was not interested in that. "I don't need that stuff and I don't want it."

He said, "Well, you might try it you might like it, and I'll give you 5 bucks. The only stipulation is that you have to have a chew in your mouth every time I'm around you."

I thought, well, 5 bucks is no chump change. I finally said, "I think I'll just take you up on the deal." So he handed me a full can of Skoal and I put a dip in my mouth.

I was going up to my combine and got to where I was getting ready to load the combine on my truck, I got so dizzy I almost, well, it's a wonder I didn't drop that combine off the side of that truck. So after a week he came up to me, and he handed me a $5.00 bill and I thought, well, at least the guy is honest, he didn't back out on the deal.

Then he asked, "What are you going to do when that can runs empty?"

I said, "I'm not going to do anything. I just did this to get your $5.00."

He said, "I'll tell you what. The first thing you'll do is, you'll go down to the grocery store and buy yourself another can."

You know, he was right. Fifty-some years later, I'm still chewing the stuff.

Running Out of Chew in Oklahoma

I'll never forget the time we were going down through the hills of Oklahoma. I was driving ole Big Red with a combine pulling a header trailer. I was following my uncle and had no idea where we were going. He'd never told me. He didn't even draw us a little map or anything, said just to follow him.

So, as I was following him, I suddenly realized that I was out of chewing tobacco. Panic started to set in, so I thought well, I've got to find a place where I can buy another can of chewing tobacco. There's got to be a bar or a gas station somewhere around here. All of a sudden I see this old bar. I pulled up where there was a nice place to pull in, shut the motor off, ran in, and asked the lady bartender if she had any Skoal chewing tobacco.

She said, "Yeah, I got one can left."

I said, "Give it to me."

She reached up on the shelf, sat it on the bar, and I asked how much. She said, "Twenty-five cents."

I threw a quarter down on the bar and went racing out to my truck as fast as I could because if I'd lost sight of my uncle up the road I don't know what I would have done. I knew I had to take a chance because I was having a "nicotine fit", I guess you'd call it.

I put the truck in gear and took off. Within a couple of miles I looked over the hill and I saw my uncle's truck, trailer, and combine. I thought, well, that's cool. Then I took my fingernail and opened up that can of Skoal. I was so happy! When I opened up that Skoal and looked down, all there was of that can was a ball about the size of a small marble. That chewing tobacco had to have been sitting on that shelf for probably years. All of it had dried up into one little ball. I thought, well, if that isn't the luck!

Apache, Oklahoma, Hotel

About the second or third year on the harvest crew, we were going through central Oklahoma. We left Temple two or three hours before the sun was getting ready to set. My uncle indicated that we could make it up the road to this town by the time it was too dark to keep going. We got as far as Apache, Oklahoma. We pulled in there and back then, there were two old hotels in that little town, if you can believe that. They were both still open.

My uncle and his cronies decided to walk up to the hotel on the north end of Main Street. My brother and I, we decided to go check the other hotel, which was right across the street. My brother thought that we probably wouldn't rent a room there, but decided we should check it out anyway.

That place was dark, and hot and dusty! We rang the little bell for service, and all of a sudden, down the steps came this Indian gal. She was about as wide as she was tall. She asked if she could help us and we said we might want to rent a room for the night.

She said, "I've got a room if you want to look at it."

"Well, what kind of rate you do have on these rooms?" we asked.

She said, "Oh, I get 50 cents a night for them." I looked at my brother and he looked at me and you know back then, that was even dirt cheap! Then she said, "Come on up. The room's on the second floor. I've got to find a light bulb before you can check out the room." She came out with, I'd say, a 25-watt light bulb. She asked my brother if he'd stand on a chair and screw it into the outlet. So he did and the light came on. We told her we'd take the room.

Boy was it hot and muggy in there. We opened the windows and tried to get a little breeze going through it.

That evening my brother said, "Jim, tomorrow we're going to be close to home again and I was wondering if you would give me a haircut." So, I got my clippers out of my grip, plugged them in with the 25-watt light bulb on. I started cutting his hair and thought I was doing alright. "Well, I'll just check it out in the morning," he said. "I'm sure you did fine."

So, that night I had to get up and use the bathroom, stepped on the floor and it was so warped that I stumbled and fell into the cardboard closet and pretty much destroyed one of the doors on the closet.

The next morning, we went outside into the light, and my brother looked in the mirror on the truck and he yelled, "Jim! Jim! What did you do to my hair?"

I said, "I'm sorry, but you know it was pretty dark in that room."

He said, "I'm going to have to go to a real barber shop when I get back home to get it straightened out."

I agreed. I sure did a number on his hair.

Brother Pat and Big Red

Losing Sleep at the Patterson Hotel

One evening, we pulled into Harper, Kansas, which was the county seat. The county seats in Kansas pretty much all had their little three story flat painted hotels in the middle of the town somewhere. So we pulled in, went over to a restaurant to get a bite to eat.

The waitress asked, "Hey, don't you boys always stay at the old Patterson Hotel when you come into town?"

We said, "Yes, we do."

She went on to say, "You're in for a surprise. Old man Patterson died last winter. He willed his hotel over to his granddaughter, who lived out in Greenwich Village in New York. A real hippie part of New York City. The first thing she did was come back and paint the whole hotel a bright pink, and renamed it the Rosalea's Hotel. That probably made every newspaper in the state of Kansas."

We went ahead and finished eating, walked around the corner and sure enough, there's the old Patterson Hotel a bright pink. We walked in and met the gal, and yeah, she was a genuine New York hippie all right. She had taken most of the doors off and put beads in place of the doors. She had incense burning everywhere. She even had an old claw foot bathtub that she put in the middle of the lobby and had filled it full of flowers. She totally hippie-fied the place, which I thought was kind of cool, actually.

We rented a room, went upstairs, and my brother told me, "Jim, I'm going to bed."

I said, "I'm going back over to the pool hall and shoot a couple of games of pool with some of the locals, and have me a couple of beers."

"Well," he said, "only one thing. If you come back to this room all liquored up, you're not staying here tonight."

I said, "Nah, don't worry about it."

So, I went over and had a few beers. When I came back and went upstairs, the door was locked. I hollered, "Pat, let me in."

Pat said, "No. I told you you're not staying here tonight if you come back all beered up."

I asked, "Where am I supposed to sleep?"

"I don't know. I guess that's your problem isn't it."

So, I went downstairs, went around to the back of the building and saw the fire escape and I said to myself, I'll just go up this fire escape, open up that window to our room and crawl in, and so that's what I did. I started to open up the window and Pat politely came over and shut the window and locked it.

I said, "Hey, I gotta get inside and get to sleep."

Pat was having none of it. He said, "No, you're not sleeping here tonight." So I thought, well, what am I going to do?

So, I went back down the fire escape, went into the lobby of the hotel and saw that claw foot bathtub with that laid-back back to it, and I said to myself, emergencies call for emergency measures. I just pulled all the flowers out of that tub, crawled in and went to sleep. The next morning there were people walking around the lobby of the hotel, laughing and pointing over at me in the bathtub, but, it didn't seem to bother me.

Getting Drunk with Merle

We had wheat to cut on the west side of Harper, which was kind of up in the hill country where the ground was all terraced and unfit to be broken out for farm ground. This old man, his name was Merle. He was the sweetest ole guy, and he lived there. Anyway, my uncle took his three combines out on the east side of Harper to another farmer where the ground was all nice and level. He'd send me and my old truck out to the west side of Harper to cut wheat on Merle's farm. This one year we had been cutting, there were mud holes everywhere. I was sliding on the terraces and it scared the living you-know-what out of me.

We finally got finished with the last load of wheat and Merle, instead of taking it into the elevator, he wanted to put it into his little tiny granary for seed wheat. It was no problem. We proceeded to pull into this old granary and we had a 2- or 3-inch electric auger that transferred the wheat into the granary. We were sitting there; it was hotter than blazes, shooting the bull.

Pretty soon, Merle said, "Are you thirsty?"

I said, "Yeah, I am kind of thirsty."

So he reached up in the rafters of that little granary and pulled out a pint of blackberry brandy. We were sipping on this brandy while we were loading that wheat into that granary. The next thing you know, I was getting pretty tipsy and I lost track of time.

By the time I got back to Harper, my uncle had already gotten his combines loaded and was ready to take off north. He came over and opened up the door of my truck and I almost fell out. He was so mad at me! I don't blame him, but he said, "I'm not waiting around, not helping you load your combine. You're on your own. We're headed north." Somehow, I got my combine loaded and was able to head north the next morning.

Jim outside of a Montana motel

Getting Ready for Nebraska

When we finished cutting wheat there at home, we had to spend a day washing our combine, trucks and stuff down because if you crossed into Nebraska with a speck of some noxious weed, they would fine you into oblivion. Another rule they had was you couldn't have more than 20 gallons of fuel on board or they'd fine you. It was the fuel tax that they would be losing out on, so they'd fine you. So, before we'd load up, we'd always go out there and make sure the fuel in the combines were down about as low as we could get it, safely; same way as the farm trucks. That way when you put that combine up on the farm truck, they'd come up there with their little sticks, stick them down in the tanks, and make sure you didn't have more than their limit of fuel in those tanks.

Well, 20 gallons of fuel isn't all that much when you've got a combine and truck. I remember a few times when we had to siphon the gas out on the ground. That was a whole lot better than getting a fine, so that's what we'd do. To this day, I have a real hard spot in my heart for the State of Nebraska in general just the way they were. I know there's just some of the most wonderful people in the world that live in Nebraska and I'm not against those wonderful people, but the State itself, well I can't imagine what it would be like today – 50 years later – it would be impossible, I imagine.

67

Pat and Ace washing the combine

Close Call in Nebraska

I'll never forget the time I was sickling right along cutting wheat between Grant and Imperial Nebraska, when the combine comes to a complete stop, which almost threw me into the steering wheel. The main fly wheel shaft broke and shredded three of the big main drive belts. I looked over to my left and saw the big fly wheel running down the stubble. I thought, wow, this has got to be serious! My brother came up, I got off the combine and we took a look at it. He said that I should take old Big Red into Imperial with the load of wheat and he would start tearing this thing apart. I thought, well, that suits me just fine.

I got in the truck, pulled up to the gate, hit the brakes and it didn't seem like there was any brakes on Big Red. I asked my brother, "How do you stop this thing?"

He said, "You just have to drag your foot."

I thought it must be all right, or he wouldn't let me take off toward Imperial with a totally unsafe truck. My younger brother decided to ride with me and we took off, got down where we saw a stop sign. There was a "T" in the road, you either had to go left or right and so I started pumping the brakes. The more I pumped the faster I went, so I started shifting down, and then realized I didn't have any brakes at all. I wasn't going to be able to stop!

I pulled clear over to the left, tried to round the corner the best I could, and I did, but I spilled wheat over the side of the truck. That truck was up on two wheels and I noticed there was a semi coming and he saw that I was going to spill something on the south side, so he pulled clear over almost in the ditch, to give me all the room he could.

Somehow I didn't tip that truck right over in front of him. I got around the corner, and coasted to a stop. I put it in low gear and ran down the shoulder of the road to the Coop in Imperial. I pulled in there and the guy came out and asked if he could help me.

I said, "I don't know. I don't have any brakes."

He crawled under the truck, and said, "Well, no wonder you don't have any brakes. You have a pin hole in your brake line and it let all your brake fluid out." That was a hair-raising experience for sure!

Rushville, Nebraska, Wheat Disaster

One year, when I was about 17 I suppose, we were headed from northern Colorado up to Glendive, Montana. We made it as far as Rushville, Nebraska. We pulled in front of a café and got out of the truck. All of a sudden, here comes this young farmer in his old pickup. He got out and went over to my uncle and said, "Hey, you've got about 3 or 4 combines there. I've got 80 acres about 5 miles west of town that I need cut in the worst way. It's been ripe for about two weeks and I can't find a combine anywhere."

My uncle had to politely tell him that we were on our way to Montana, and we need to get up there. We should have been up there yesterday, and we wouldn't be able to help him out.

The poor guy pleaded with my uncle. Finally my uncle said, "Jim, why don't you just go unload your machine and go cut the 80 acres. You can catch up with us in a couple of days."

I said, "Okay." I unloaded my combine, put the header on it and headed to the wheat field out west of Rushville. I pulled into the gate and looked at the field of wheat and thought, my goodness this is probably 50- to 60-bushel wheat, it was so thick and lush; and that farmer, that poor guy, he was just so happy, almost had tears in his eyes. He was telling me that this field of wheat was going to pull him out of debt and he was going to buy his kids some presents.

So, I started around the field backwards, and I got about 50 yards I suppose, and I looked around in the bin and there wasn't any wheat coming into the machine. I thought, oh no, maybe I left the elevator door hanging down or something. The wheat must be going out on the ground. So, I stopped and I jumped off my combine and he came walking up there and said, "What's wrong?"

I said, "Well, I don't know, but there's no wheat coming into the bin."

Charlie Thompson, Uncle Mike and Joe Willie Thompson adjusting combine sieves

So we got to scratching around on the back of the combine and found some wheat kernels and they were just hollow, they were like chaff. He proceeded to tell me that they had gotten a hard freeze on that field just at the wrong time when it was still green, that's why the heads didn't really have anything in them. I just felt so bad for that guy. I'll never forget that. So I pulled up and took the combine back into Rushville. I loaded it back on Big Red and headed up to Montana the next morning.

Going To the Dogs

One year after we finished cutting wheat in northeastern Colorado, we took off north, headed for Glendive, our next stop. We made it as far as downtown Rapid City before it got too dark to keep on going. We rented a hotel room. We probably weren't in there five minutes, came back out and our suitcases were gone! I remember thinking to myself, well, they couldn't have gotten too far in that short of time so I took off down the sidewalk in front of the business district buildings.

All of a sudden, out of the shadows came a couple of guys. They were probably 6'6" and one of them came up to me and pulled out a knife. One of the guys said, "I think maybe you just better give me your billfold."

I kept looking at that knife, and thought I'd rather lose my billfold than my life, so I handed it over to him and went back to the hotel and told them what happened.

My uncle's partner, he was from Oklahoma, he was pretty disgusted that they stole his suitcase. "Well," he said. "Let's all jump in the pickup and go out to the dog track. Might as well get this all behind us somehow. Maybe we'll go out there and win some money."

We all jumped into the pickup and headed out to the dog track. When we got there, I didn't know anything about dog races, so I took the program and looked through it. I saw a dog by the name of Kansas Kit. I didn't know any more about Kansas Kit than the rest of the dogs, so I pulled out the $2.00 I still had in my pocket and placed a bet on that dog. They took off and ran around the track. Coming down the back stretch I thought I saw about seven or eight dogs all bunched up. There was this one dog about 50 yards behind all the rest. He must have been sick or something. I noticed that it was Kansas Kit. That day, I had no luck whatsoever.

Truck Inspections in Wibaux

After we finished combining in Peetz, Colorado, we headed toward Montana. We always had wheat to cut up there. First, Glendive, then from there we'd go up on the Canadian border to a little town called Wolf Point, Montana. If I can remember right, it's on the Indian reservation up there. Anyway, this one year, we pulled into this little town called Wibaux, just off the Interstate. I'd say a mile down the road to the west was a weigh station.

This particular year, my brother and I built a header trailer to put the head of the combine on, and we "scabbed" a car frame together which made it really, really heavy.

So, when we got to the weigh station the guy looked out his window at my old truck and my header trailer and he said, "That header trailer looks pretty heavy. I think you better drive across my scale." So I did. Then he said, "That thing weighs about 200 lbs more than a single-axle trailer should weigh."

I said, "I don't know what to do about it."

He said, "Well, I'm gonna just let you go this time, but you need to figure out something a little lighter."

"Okay", I said.

And then he looked at my truck and trailer and he said, "I'm going to give you a safety inspection on your outfit before you take off."

So, he got out in front of my truck, and he said, "Turn on your left turn signal." I put on my left turn signal. Of course, there was nothing. When you run around in a wheat field, your wires get caught up in this and that. Wires get broken and your lights, half of them don't work. He said, "Turn on your right turn signal." He came around and opened up the door of my truck and he said, "I want to see you hit the brakes." So I did. Of course, those old vacuum brakes, you have to pump them at least 3 or 4 times before you get any kind of peddle. So he went around back and said, "Hit your brakes. Sorry, there's no brake light. Hit your left turn signal." Nothing! "Hit your right turn signal." Nothing! He came around and he said to me, "You know, I've got a notion to red-flag this piece of junk that you're trying to run up and down our highway."

I said, "Well, I don't know about that. I've got to get north of Glendive and get to cutting wheat."

He said "I'm going to give you a warning. There's a mechanic shop there just this side of Glendive, and I want you to pull in and get all this stuff taken care of before you go any farther."

"Yes, sir, I will. Don't worry." So he wrote me a warning ticket and I put it in my glove box. I then took off.

The last thing on my mind was getting anything fixed on that truck with limited money and I needed to get to making money. I remember seeing that shop as I drove by. We finished cutting wheat in Glendive, then went on up to Wolf Point and cut up there.

Now it was time for school to start. I called up my Dad, and I said, "Dad, school's starting. I need to get home."

He said, "You know, winter's coming and we need the money, Jim. Why don't you stay and keep cutting."

"Okay, I'll stay a little longer." Well, about a week went by and I called him up and I said, "Dad, am I a week late for school now?"

He said, "Jim, you need to stay up there and keep cutting."

"Dad, I'm going to give you a choice. I can either come home on my own, or come home with this truck and combine."

He said, "Well, I guess just go ahead and come home then."

My uncle came in and says, "Are you going to get the brakes and stuff fixed before you head home?"

I said, "Well, there's a problem. I don't have the money and I don't have the time."

He said, "Well, good luck then!" So I took off.

I got a room at the Jordan and told them that I needed a wakeup call for about 5:00 in the morning. I needed to figure a way to get past those scales out there a mile west of Wibaux on the Interstate. Maybe if I got an early start they might not be open yet.

So I took off and crept around Glendive in the dark. Got out there on the Interstate close enough to where the sun was trying to creep up a little. I was squinting to see if the scale sign said "open" or "closed" and it said "closed." That made me feel like I was halfway home.

I took the Wibaux exit and noticed the lights were on at the café. Oh, no, there's a cop car sitting there. So I shut my lights off and the motor off and figured I would just coast by and no one would notice me. I got about a mile out of town and all of a sudden here's this red light.

I pull over. The guy comes walking up. I thought, oh my goodness, this might not turn out too well because that's the same guy that gave me that warning ticket 30 days before. He came up and he said, "The reason I pulled you over is because the combine tires are too wide."

I said, "If I need to see what's behind me I just take the steering wheel, turn it a little to the left and I can see everything I need to."

He just kind of shook his head and then said, "Well, I need to give you a safety check on your truck." So he got out, and said, "Let's see your left turn signal." Nothing! "Turn on your right turn signal." Nothing! Came around, "Hit your brakes." Same thing, so he went around back. "Turn your left signal on." Nothing! He came up and said "Where are you heading?"

"I'm heading home. I'm a week late for school."

And he said, "Well, I've got a notion to just red-flag this piece of crap you're driving, and you'll have to call a mechanic out of town to get all this taken care of." But then he said, "You know, there's a mechanic shop 30 miles down the road. I'm going to let you go. I'm going to give you a warning ticket, but you've gotta get all this stuff fixed."

"No problem, officer." He gave me a warning ticket and I took off like a bullet.

I reached into the glove box, grabbed my other warning ticket and started comparing them. The only thing different was the date on them. I just couldn't help it. I wadded them up together and pitched them out the window, laughing for a few miles down the road. Made me feel like a bird that had just been released from its cage. To this day, I have never figured out whether or not that cop recognized me that second time around, or just let me go because he understood my situation.

Hair Cutting and Barber Shop Stories

When I was about 7 or 8 years old, my mom got tired of cutting my hair and I got tired of her cutting it because she wasn't the greatest barber in the world. She'd always say when she got done, "Well, Jim, the only difference between a good haircut and a bad one is about three days."

My little buddy and I used to go down to the barber shop. A regular haircut was 35 cents and a flattop was 50 cents. So we sat in the chair and the barber would work on our hair for a little while, and then he'd say, "How does that look?" "Well," I said, "could you make it a little bit flatter on the top?" So, he would, and we were able to get by with a 35 cent haircut, instead of paying the 50 cents. He probably knew we were pulling a fast one over on him.

Another haircutting story was when we were cutting wheat in Cut Bank, Montana. The harvest crew all went into the barber shop at the same time. As my brother was getting his hair cut, one of the winos came in and asked the barber if he could have a shot of his hair tonic. Of course, the barber thought he was probably just kidding, so he told him, "No problem. You've got the bottle of your choice." So, to everyone's surprise, the old wino got up, unscrewed the cap, and proceeded to drink the hair tonic right down. Now, that's what you call being hard up for a drink!

When I was about 16, and got home from Montana, I needed a hair cut in the worst way. I was about a week late for high school, so I rushed down to the local barbershop, sat down in the chair, and he asked me how I wanted it cut. I told him to leave it about a half inch long on the sides and back. He got done, turned me back around so I could see myself in his big mirror. He'd shaved my sides. I looked so silly! I went to school and realized he did the same stunt to a couple of my buddies. I told them I would open up my own barbershop in our upstairs bathroom. The barber got wind of his competition, so he offered a reward for a picture of me practicing haircutting and not being licensed. I cut three or four heads of hair and got his attention before I gave up the whole thing.

World War II Heroes

My uncle, being a WWII veteran himself, always tried to make it a point to hire the vets because he had a real soft spot for those down and out guys. He'd hire them when nobody else would. I remember there was one man called Bodock. He was such an alcoholic, but you know, deep down, he had a heart of gold and my uncle would hire him every summer.

I remember one time we were going through central Oklahoma on the way back, after we finished cutting wheat on the Texas-Oklahoma border. There was a guy standing along the road. My uncle stopped and said, "Hey, you looking for work?"

"Yeah, I sure am," the man said.

My uncle ended up hiring him. Yes, the man was also an alcoholic. My uncle would look past it somehow and hire these guys anyway. I had to give my uncle a lot of credit for his compassion for men down on their luck. I also remember that the man's girlfriend was very short and plump. She had to tie a short 2x4 on the gas pedal of their old clunker of a car so she could reach it.

Dad's Embarrassing Attendance

I grew up with two older brothers. One was four years older and one was six years older than me. They were heavily involved in sports: basketball and football. So I was always playing basketball with them at a very, very young age. By the time I started grade school I was a pretty good basketball player. I made the starting team in sixth grade. When I was in high school, I was playing on the varsity team, on Friday nights.

All week my dad would be hauling grain mostly to Kansas City, and by the time Friday night came around, he was dead tired. So, we'd be playing the game, he'd come walking in half lit. He'd sit down on the end of the subs bench, like it was no big thing. I just felt so bad for the guy because he wanted to come and see his boy play a game. Sometimes he'd go up in the bleachers and lie down and take a nap. It was pretty embarrassing, but it was something I never really blamed him for because I knew his situation.

Halloween Hoodlums

Halloween was always a big night. During those high school years, it was so much fun. We'd soap car windows, what have you. I remember this one guy had a car, pulled it up on his yard right out in front where it had a porch light on. He just knew that his car was safe because nobody would dare crawl up on his yard and mess with his car. Well, we didn't want to stay up all night, so we crawled up one time and were going to let the air out of his tires.

All of a sudden, the lights flashed a couple times so we went scurrying out of there. Well, you know, we can't let this guy win. We waited 'til about 11 o'clock, I suppose. We crawled up there again and loosened the valve stem on his back tire and ran off to watch it go flat on him. Thought that was the most hilarious thing we could imagine. We won! His tire went flat. He knew that his car was totally safe, parked up that close to his house. We were just a couple of young, radical guys, bound and determined to win out. And we did!

"The ultimate goal of farming is not the growing of crops, but the cultivation and perfection of human beings." Masanobu Fukuoka

Taking Driving Lessons

I remember we had this old, about a 1952, panel wagon that the school used for a Driver's Education car. You could pile about five or six kids in it, plus the instructor. He had a brake over there on the passenger side, so everything was cool. Never forget the time I was driving, going up Blueberry Hill and there was a bunch of pot holes in the road. It was probably in the spring before they got around to throwing a little bit of asphalt in them. Secretly, I'm looking for the deepest pot hole, thinking it'd be funny if I rode over the deepest one. So, I'm trying to get the instructor to think that I'm watching for pot holes to avoid them. Of course, I hit the deepest one. Oh, my goodness, the dirt just flew out of the headliner on that old car. Everybody thought it was funny. All the kids knew what I was up to and I'm sure the Driver's Ed instructor did too.

Last Day Party

Sometimes people get into being school teachers that really shouldn't be school teachers. They just don't have what it takes to keep control of the kids in the classes. We had a Spanish teacher like that. Sweetest guy in the world, but he couldn't control his classes at all. The classes would get out of hand.

So, one time a couple weeks before the school was to get out in the spring, he said, "I'm going to treat all of you kids to some kind of treat at the last day of school."

So, he went around and asked everybody what kind of pop they wanted him to buy for them. Of course most people said Pepsi or Coke or whatever.

Me and my buddy, we wanted to play a game with the guy. I told him, "You know, the only kind of pop I can drink is Red Bird."

He said, "Well, I don't know if there's any Red Bird pop around."

I said, "If you can't find a Red Bird, then don't buy me one."

Later, I found out that he drove all the way up into Nebraska and finally found an old time grocery store that had Red Bird pop in it. Later I got to thinking, well, that wasn't too funny. I used to be such a jackass.

Cutting Kitties on Main Street

In the winter time, when I was in high school, I had a good buddy and we'd always cruise up and down Main Street at night after having a few beers. This one night, I remember driving down to the bottom of Main Street, turning around, and we'd come screaming up Main Street. There wasn't a soul out that night, and the street was pretty much deserted. The night watchman, he was over at City Hall. He had seen us go up Main Street, probably 10 miles over the speed limit, I guess. We'd go up, make a U-turn and head back down Main Street. He came out, waited for us to make a U-turn. We'd come screaming back up Main Street. He would stand there, trying to flag us down. Of course, we just went around him, laughing and having a good time. Go down, turn around, make a U-turn, and head back up.

After a while of this, he was getting more aggressive. He was using both hands trying to get us to stop. Of course we didn't, we just went down, turned around, and came back. Well, the next time he got his gun out. He was a little more serious, and waved his gun at us. We just went down and made another U-turn. We went screaming back up, but this time, he fired off his gun a couple times. I remember looking in my rear view mirror seeing the flash from the barrel of the gun going off. I told my buddy, "Well, I think we'd better call it a night." So, we headed home. We were a couple of young misfits, that's all.

Big Red's New Motor

It got to be late August up on the Canadian border and most of the school kids would go home, so my uncle would have to go into town and try to hire truck drivers to haul the wheat to the bins. All he could ever find was old winos, so he'd have to hire them.

That last year that I can remember up there, we were out cutting about 11 o'clock in the morning. My uncle crawled up on my combine and told me, "Bodock and the other wino are both too drunk to let them drive the trucks, even here in the field. When you get your combine full and Big Red is full of wheat, just shut your combine off and take it to the bin. I can't trust these guys to be driving these trucks." So, I did.

I crawled in Big Red, put it in low and got ready to take off. For some reason, I thought, "I wonder where old Bodock is?" So I shut the motor off, walked around the truck and there he was — up under the tires, in the shade, passed out. Why I didn't run right over him, to this day I'll never know, but I didn't.

I remember one time, I looked across the prairie, and there was this one old wino driving Big Red and driving like a maniac that I thought he was going to tear that truck to pieces. Big Red's motor was running bad and went through the oil. When I got ready to take it home, I bought a case of oil. It got to be where I wouldn't even stop to check the oil. I'd just dump in 2 quarts of oil about every 40 miles. That was how bad the motor was getting.

But the next spring, we had to do something with that motor, overhaul it or replace it. So my dad went down with a load of wheat to Kansas City, stopped at a junk yard in Lawrence and bought a motor. Only problem was it was an overhead valve motor and the motor in Big Red was a flat head. My brother and I took our little trailer and went down and got it and brought it home. We asked our dad, "Dad, will this motor bolt up?"

"Oh, yeah, it will bolt up just fine," he said. "You won't have any problems."

We took the truck out to the old neighbor guy, threw a log chain across the branch of a tree and pulled the motor out. First thing I noticed was that the motor from the junk yard only had one hose connected on top to the radiator, one on the bottom. The radiator that was in there had two on top and two on the bottom. So we had to solder a couple ports shut. The clutch assembly was totally different, so my brother got under there and somehow welded a clutch mechanism that seemed to work, so we got ready to put the motor in.

Problem was, the filter on the newer motor was on the bottom so when we tried to put the motor in, the filter was too long. I went into Concordia and got a little shorter filter and screwed that in. It was short enough to where we could put the motor in. I asked my brother, "How's anybody ever gonna change that filter? It's right up against the steering column down there."

He just said, "Well, I guess that filter will never get changed again, now will it?"

About that time, my brother got drafted and was on his way to the Service. So, I took Big Red and the combine and headed south. I was going down the Interstate down by Salina, bucking the south wind. The motor needed to be tuned up and it really didn't have much power. I'm going down the Interstate about 30 mph, as fast as I could go.

Pretty soon this cop comes up and pulls me over and he says, "Minimum speed on this Interstate is 45 mph, and I clocked you going 28, so here's your ticket. Now, you need to get this piece of junk off my Interstate. The next exit down there, I want you to take that gravel road."

I asked, "Where's it going?"

He says, "I have no idea, but you're not going to be driving down my Interstate under the minimum speed limit."

So I took it, went down the gravel road, ended up back on the Interstate a few miles down.

Got down to Oklahoma and cut wheat down there. I got all the way back to Harper, Kansas, and was out cutting on Merle's field. I pulled into the elevator and the elevator guy says, "Well, you sure got a bad leak under your truck." I went out and looked, and sure enough the oil filter had rubbed up against the steering column enough to grind a hole in it. I had to get some of the locals to fix a by-pass filter, a little shorty. It couldn't hold a filter, but at least it let the oil flow and it wouldn't leak anymore. So that's how we solved that problem.

Life's Major Wake Up Call

The old saying "Tomorrow is promised to no one" really hit home to me Christmas Eve when I was 17. I lost my perfectly healthy mother from a massive stroke. My dad pretty much lost his senses after that for a few years, and left me to pretty much finish raising my 13-year old sister and my 16-year old brother. Thankfully, there was a junior college 11 miles away that I was able to afford and attend after high school, and I was able to live at home and look after my siblings. Had those events not happened, I probably would have ended up in Vietnam like so many of my friends. Sometimes we don't always see or understand the bigger picture.

"We raised our kids the best we could, doing what we loved to do. It was hard work, but we always had time to smile and laugh." Thomas Meyer

Celebrating In the Wrong Place

On my 18th birthday my buddy said to me, "Let's go to a big town and celebrate your birthday up right." So, we jumped in his car and headed off to Salina, about 50 miles south. Found a little 3.2 bar with pool tables that served pizza and beer. We went in there and ordered a pizza and a pitcher of beer, played a couple games of pool. I got to feeling sick, so I told my buddy, "Let's go. This really isn't fun." So he agreed.

We were walking down the ramp out of the place, and one of the Salina cops was coming up the ramp, took one look at me and asked my buddy what was wrong with me. My buddy said, "He just doesn't feel good. He probably has the flu."

The cop said, "Well, we got places for guys like him." He came over and threw the cuffs on me and away we go to the jail downtown.

They put me in this jail cell that was like a dungeon. For a bed, it had a piece of steel held up by 2 chains. No pillow, no sheets, middle of winter, it was cold as you know what in there. Out of the dark shadows came this guy. He had about a foot-long beard, long hair, scared the living you-know-what out of me. He knew I was scared. He said, "I'm sorry, I didn't mean to scare you," and he walked back into the darkness. Last I ever saw of him. My neighbor lady bailed me out the next day. I went to court and got a fine for public drunkenness. On my 18th birthday — what an ordeal!

Trading Combines

The 1963 John Deere 55 combine that I cut my eye-teeth on ran for six or seven summers. After that much grain going through the thing, it was just wore out. Everything on it was worn out. We had to put patches of tin on the sides and tape them on to keep the grain from going through the metal that was worn through. Poor thing just couldn't go anymore on a harvest. So, my dad and I had to sit down and decide what we were going to do. He said "Well, let's go down to Minneapolis, Kansas. I know a John Deere Dealer down there a little bit, and we'll see if maybe we can trade the combine for a little better used machine."

We went down there, and the guy had a 1967 John Deere 95, 20-foot header, instead of a 14-foot header. We're sitting there and finally we said, "Well, how much money are you going to have to trade?" The man said, "Well, for the 55, I can probably allow you $2,000.00 on a trade. I want $6,000.00 for this machine. So we can trade for $4,000.00."

I told my dad, "Don't you think you should tell this guy how worn out our combine is, because when he goes up to pick it up, he might just be beside himself when he sees the patches on the side of the machine where we had to tape metal to keep the grain from coming out. It's just worn out."

Dad turned to me and says, "Yeah, I think we'd better tell him. Better let him know before we finalize this deal, because we don't want him to be shocked when he goes to pick up that machine up in Jamestown."

So we told him. "Hey, we got to let you know that '55 is totally worn out."

The guy says, "You know, I've seen lots of used combines, don't worry about it."

To this day I think he realized he was dealing with a WWII Veteran that was basically broke anyway, and he wanted to try to help the poor old guy out as much as he could. There still are some really decent people out there.

My $70 Combine

I became good friends with a lady that lived near Jamestown. She had three or four kids and a very, very alcoholic husband who was a WWII vet. She was always inviting me out, trying to get me and her daughter together. She was a very sweet young lady, but I wasn't that much interested in her. With the lady's husband being such an alcoholic, they were pretty much sliding into debt, so she finally had to have an auction of the farm equipment to pay bills.

I went out to the farm auction and they had an old International combine. I got to looking it over and I was like a chicken on a June bug looking that thing over because it looked like such a brand new combine. It didn't even have the paint worn off the auger. I thought maybe I could buy the thing. When the auction came around to the combine, I ended up buying it for $70. To this day I believe everyone there stopped bidding on it because they must have known how badly I wanted that combine. It was an older machine, but very little grain had gone through it, probably a few acres actually. So, I thought I'd start running that combine on at least my uncle's wheat, he could pay me, and I could make some money.

That particular summer we were cutting wheat around the Jamestown area. I told my dad that I was going to run my machine and he was going to have to find somebody else to run his machine. I jumped on my "new" International and was out cutting my uncle's wheat. That thing would keep up with those John Deeres, it was no problem. I was so happy! But all of a sudden, the main drive belt came apart.

So I parked the combine, and I went down to Concordia to the International Dealer. I walked in with the old belt, put it on the counter and the man went into the back and got a new one. He set it on the counter, and I asked, "How much?"

He said, "$120.00."

"$120.00? I only gave $70 for the whole combine!"

He said, "That doesn't have anything to do with the price of the belt. If you got that combine for free, this belt would still be $120.00." So I went ahead and bought it, went out and put it on, and got the combine started.

It cut for about another hour or two, but when I looked back, steam was coming out of the radiator. The top of the radiator had rusted through. So, I just parked my combine again, got back on my dad's combine, and that was the end of my $70 Combine days.

A Little Scratch Never Hurt Anything

One night I was out drinking with one of my best buddies. He was the second "gutter brother" of mine. Three of us were nicknamed "The Gutter Brothers" by our classmates. When we came home, my tractor and the tandem disk were parked on the street in front of our house. He cut it too close and took out the passenger side of his folk's car.

I remember him telling me that the damage won't affect the way the car would go down the road or how it would ride, so it really wasn't any big deal at all. I thought, "I hope your folks think it isn't a very big deal either when you show them what you did to the side of their car." Guess what? I remember his folks were angry about their car, and rightly so, but I don't recall what kind of punishment they gave to my buddy.

Short Love

When I was about 17, whenever we were cutting wheat up in Glendive, Montana, we stayed in the old part of the Jordan Hotel. We would come in at night and I'd meet up with this little Italian gal who worked at the hotel. She was a beautiful young gal. She'd always be waiting for me. I thought, well maybe she's the one. I told her that when I got back from Wolf Point, which would be about 28 to 30 days before we'd finish cutting the wheat, I'd come back to Glendive and we'd start where we left off. She agreed.

Long about late August, we had finished cutting the wheat, so I headed down to the Jordan Hotel. I went in and asked the lady behind the desk if Connie was still working there. The lady said no, and that she got married about two weeks before. She didn't live there anymore, and that her new husband was in the Air Force. Maybe that wasn't meant to be true love after all.

Up in Montana

Up in Montana, I had a little blond girlfriend. I was 18 at the time. She was 17. One night she says, "Let's go climb the water tower." I'm like, boy that sounds kind of scary to me. I wasn't going to chicken out. She took off up the ladder of the water tower. She had on a pair of white shorts. Let your imagination run with that one. So we got up on the water tower. She laid down on the grates and wanted to make out. I didn't think that would be much fun on those grates, so I told her no. Long story short, she basically told me in no uncertain terms to take a hike. That was the end of that relationship. Nothing like a woman's scorn.

Not So Sly

The last year of the harvest, my dad went along with me. We had just the one machine and two trucks. He wanted to go on the harvest one more time. So I agreed to go one more year so he could make one more harvest run. When we got up to Wolf Point, Montana, after we had cut wheat all day, he said, "Jim, let's go across the street and have a drink or two."

So we walked over to the bar. There was this girl dancing in a cage, and as we sat there, she kept giving me the eye. She was a pretty, hot looking girl.

Next morning, I woke up and looked out the window. My dad was walking around in the parking lot, wondering where the heck I was. After a short interrogation, we were able to get about the business of the day.

Real Love

One of the worst things about being on the harvest crew from the age of 14 through 23 was that you'd be in a town for a week to 10 days, usually cutting wheat, and then you'd move on. It was a way to meet a lot of nice, wonderful people, but the one thing that was hard to deal with was you'd meet some young gal and basically fall in love. I believe that's what most young folks are looking for. They're looking for love. After a week or 10 days, you'd fall head over heels for some gal, and then it would be time to go along to the next town and start the cycle all over again. It was really hard to deal with. My heart goes out to these young people who are looking for love of any kind. It can be a tough game.

Never Let a Bee Know You Fear It

When I was a kid, I had a buddy whose dad owned the hardware store and the Case Tractor store there in town. In that little town back then, every building downtown had a business in it. In the fall of the year, my buddy's dad would sponsor a plowing competition to show off his Case Tractors. The first year I remember his tractor had a five bottom plow. The next year it was a 6 bottom plow. Next year it was a 7 bottom plow. I remember my dad telling me that every time they made the tractors bigger and more powerful, it would only be a matter of time before small farmers would be a thing of the past. Boy was he spot on about that.

Anyway, as the town dried up and the hardware store had to close, a fellow from Texas rented the hardware store building and turned it into a honey bee processing plant where he would spin the honey out into 55-gallon drums. One time, he hired my dad's semi to haul a load of drums full of honey to his place in Texas. I remember when they were getting loaded, I told the man I wasn't going to come in that building with all those bees in there.

He said to me, "Jim, if the bees know you're afraid of them, they will sting you. But, if you let them know you aren't afraid of them, they will never sting you."

So I said, "Okay, I'll take your word on it." So, I went into the building. There were bees everywhere and didn't get stung once.

Before my dad headed for Texas, dad had me drag out the garden hose and wash off the honey on the drums. I'm up there in the back of that trailer and all of a sudden, a bee stung me. I proceed to bail over the side of the trailer, hit the ground running while waving my arms trying to keep the bees from stinging me as I'm running down the road. By the time I got done out-running those bees I must have got stung seven or eight more times. I thought to myself, well, just because you tell those bees you're not scared of them, they might not always believe you.

Cowbell Justice to Protect the Watermelon

One of the stories my younger brother, Kevin, liked to tell, I swear I don't remember it, but he swears up and down it happened. My dad was always hauling grain to Texas and this one time he brought back a load of watermelon. He didn't have a tarp on the load so the watermelon just sat up there where anybody and the birds could see them.

Kevin and one of his buddies were worried about somebody coming at night and crawling up the back of that trailer, heisting one of those watermelons off the back. So the story he tells is that they took some string and took a cowbell that my mother used to signal when it was suppertime when we were playing down the block. He says they took a string, tied the cowbell on it, put it on the back of the trailer and that way if somebody crawled up there to take a watermelon, they'd hit that string and that cowbell would drop. He'd hear it from his tent in the front yard.

So, the last time I saw him he swears up and down that the cowbell went off, and that me and one of my buddies was stealing a watermelon off there. It probably happened, but like I say, I can't remember it, but it doesn't mean it didn't happen.

Truck Trouble in Texas

My dad called me up from Happy, Texas (south of Amarillo). He said the motor on his semi needed to get overhauled, and wondered if I couldn't jump in the old '51 Ford and drive down there. I said that I guess I could. He then said that I probably ought to bring some money with me, which I did. I went down there and they had finished overhauling the motor. The bill was $4,200. I had been able to save up a little money and was able to get the bill paid. Shortly after that, my dad had a heart attack. So I told dad, "I'll stay out of college this last year and drive your semi because you can't."

I began hauling oats out of North Dakota to Fort Worth, Texas, going through Oklahoma City. One night, it was raining, dark, the air conditioner thing was leaking water, and the windshield was fogging over. I'm sitting there trying to wipe the condensation off the windshield, and all of a sudden the motor seizes up. Well, the old boy over in Happy, Texas, he forgot to put any Loctite on a "T" in the heater hose line. So, it drained all the water out. I hauled it over to a mechanic. Another $4,200. I gave him a nice down payment so we could get it out of hock. So, not so lucky on semis, combines, farming, you name it.

Nebraska Scales Justice

I remember the time my dad got a 10-load contract of corn out of Fairmont, Nebraska. I went up there and loaded our little 33-ft grain trailer we had and took off to the south. Before I left the house, to go up there, my dad said, "Be sure you don't overload this thing because that little scale there on the Kansas-Nebraska border is more than likely going to be open, so you don't want to run a chance of getting a ticket." So I said, "Don't worry. I won't."

I loaded up, had about 72,800 lbs on and the legal limit was 73,280, and I thought, man I hate to leave here being 500-600 lbs short. It's going to cut into the profit, but I thought better safe than sorry.

So I took off, got down the road, and sure enough the little scale was open. We weighed my steering axle, the green light comes on; driver's, green light. Weighed my trailer axles and red light, red light, red light!

Pretty soon I hear over the loud speaker, "Come in and bring your papers in."

I went in and said, "What's wrong?"

He said, "You're about 150 lbs heavy on your trailer axle back there."

I said, "Well, I'll just throw that tarp back, and grab my scoop shovel and I'll scoop some of that corn a little further up and that way it won't be over."

He said, "Nah, too late. Here's your ticket." I looked at it, $57.00! That definitely would take away any profit on that load of corn.

I went home and showed the ticket to my dad. He was not a happy camper! He didn't get real upset at me because those things happen, so we unloaded that corn. Loaded up the next day, and thought I'd better be a little more careful. I loaded the corn, tried to load it a little further to the front that way it wouldn't be overweight on that back axle.

I pulled on the scale, green light; driver, green light. Then, trailer, red, red, red! Again I hear, "Pull over and bring in all your papers." I thought, you gotta be kidding me. I walk in there and he says, "You're 50 lbs heavy on your back axle. Here's your ticket." $57.00!

I said, "I could go out there and kick a little ice off that trailer and I'd be just fine."

"Nope," he said, "too late."

So I said, "You know, I hate to be a predictor of gloom and doom for you, but if you're treating other truckers this way, some day something bad is going to happen to you."

When I had to give my dad that second ticket, he picked up the phone and cancelled the other eight loads and told me we would never haul another load out of Nebraska ever again.

It was a month or two later and I'm sitting in a truck stop, drinking a cup of coffee, and there's another trucker sitting there too. I told him what happened. He listened and pretty soon he says, "Well, Jim. You don't have to worry about that ever happening to you again. One night after the scale closed, some trucker, I assume, busted the window and threw about four sticks of dynamite in there. That little scale isn't there anymore." I thought goody, goody, goody!

Hauling Wheat to Galveston

The last year I was driving my dad's semi because he had a heart attack and couldn't drive. He got a contract for about 10 loads of wheat from Jamestown to Galveston, Texas, which was like 1600 miles round trip. Two trips a week in an old '65 Diamond T that didn't have all the power in the world. We made do with it.

Worst part of the trip was when you got south of Houston, to get over to Galveston there would be what they called the ship canal bridge. It was so steep that I would try to get as much of a run to it as I could before I'd start up that bridge. I knew that if I missed a gear I wouldn't be able to get over that bridge. When I got almost to the top, I'd get down in low gear and that poor motor would just groan. If a sparrow would have landed on the trailer of the truck, I don't think I would have had enough power to get over the top. The motor would literally go womp, womp, womp, womp. That's how close it was to running out of power, and probably running backwards. It was terrifying, it was literally terrifying. To this day, I think to myself, if that motor would have stopped right up there, I'd probably still be in jail in Houston.

Coming back from Galveston on another trip, I pulled into a truck stop in the north part of Ft. Worth. I was sitting there in my truck and all of a sudden here comes a guy, he was in an old rattle trap of a car. He gets out and comes over and says, "Hey, want to buy a gold banded diamond ring?"

I said, "Well, I don't think so."

He proceeded to take this ring out of a tray of several rings and made a little mark on the side of the wing of my truck to try to show me it was a real diamond. Of course, I was so gullible, I couldn't tell the difference between a mark and a scratch, but he was able to convince me it was a real diamond. He told me, "Well, I want to let you know that these rings are hot, but I've got a wife and four kids, and this car that needs a little gas, and I need a little something to feed the kids. I'll let you have this ring for twenty bucks." I looked at the tag on it and it said $299.00. I thought to myself, if nothing else I could be helping this family out and getting a heck of a bargain on a diamond ring. I handed him a 20 dollar bill and he took off.

I went ahead and headed home, got up the road about 100 miles, and looked at that ring on my finger and saw that my finger was turning green. I thought, oh, no, this probably wasn't real gold was it. Oh, no, it wasn't. Wasn't a real diamond either, but you know, that's how we learn I guess. Learn the hard way.

I was on the way home (that was the second trip to Galveston that week), early on a Saturday morning. I was so tired and the sun was coming up. I'm only about 40 miles from home and I'm thinking that if I could just get home and lie down on my bed everything would be fine. But I was literally so tired. I thought the farm yard lights that were on were literally coming off the farm and coming out onto the highway. That's what you'd call being too tired to drive. I got home and rested a few hours.

I went on down to the pool hall that afternoon. I was sitting there having a cold beer when my buddy that was hauling down to Galveston, too, driving his brother's semi, came in and sat down. I had that ring in my pocket, so I pulled it out and I showed it to him, and I said, "Darrell, I hate to admit it, but I really made a fool of myself by believing this ring was a $300.00 ring."

He looked at me and said, "Well, Jim, don't feel too bad." He reached into his pocket and pulled an identical looking ring out of his pocket and said, "I'm just as big a fool as you are, aren't I?" So we had a good laugh together and figured maybe we learned something from it.

Outsmarting the Grain Inspectors

In the winter, the railroad used to cut the rates on grain haulers and my dad used to say, the only reason they do this is to try to run as many truckers out of business as they could so that farmers would have to rely on the railroad.

I used to go up to North Dakota, right across the border, a little town called Ellendale. I'd load up that little 33-foot grain trailer, and the only way I could get a load on it was to have the elevator fill it until the oats were running over the sides. I'd get up and stomp and walk and jump up and down on the oats and then I'd have them put another pass down the middle. That way I could get a little more on, do that one more time, then I'd tarp it all down. The oats were spilling off the side, but I figured since we were paying 50 cents a bushel for the oats and getting a dollar a bushel for them south of Fort Worth, Texas, even though I might lose a few oats, I wasn't losing any real money.

I'd have to keep my fingers crossed going from Ellendale down to the South Dakota border because we didn't have permits to be up in North Dakota.

One time I took a load of oats down to Texas. It would take a week to go from south of Forth Worth to Ellendale and back. The grain broker indicated where I was to take my load, and those people went up there with their foot-long probes and probed a few spots of my oat load and found a few weed seeds. They turned the load down and I had to take it to another location and ended up taking a discount on it. I ended up actually losing money on that trip.

So the next trip, I thought, well, I'll just try to outsmart them. So I had my younger brother and sister help me go up on top of the load with our little bowls that we used for cereal, and we'd swirl that top foot of oats around until we couldn't see any possible seeds that weren't oat seeds. We just kept putting our little bowls in and cleaned that top layer of oats down to where you couldn't find any possible weed seeds. That's how I ended up getting around that little problem.

Tulsa Manure Back Haul

We used to haul milo down south of Fort Worth, Texas. Then we'd head all the way back to Kansas. After many loads, I said to my dad, "Why couldn't we get something to haul back north?"

He said, "There's really nothing that pays worth a darn. It was hard to get a load to bring back north."

So, one time when I was down in Fort Worth, I talked to the broker, and he said, "I can get you a load of cow manure over here at the Fort Worth stockyards. You could take that load to Tulsa. It doesn't pay all that much, but if you want to load it and head back north, I can get you some."

So, I went to the stockyard where they loaded up 50-lb sacks of cow manure. I took the load up to Tulsa and got it unloaded, then got back to I-35.

It was supposed to be a 2-day turnaround, but ended up being a 3-day ordeal. I remember going in and giving my dad a check for about $80. Of course, that trip to Ft. Worth and back with a load of milo was about $250, so when I handed him the check, I said, "Well, Dad, I guess you were right. You know more about this business than I do." I didn't pull that stunt any more.

Not What I Bargained For

I used to haul grain down south of Ft. Worth, Texas. After I'd get the grain off the trailer, I'd have to go back to Ft. Worth, hang around and wait to pick up the check from the grain broker. I'd go to a bar down on Exchange Street, not far from where they ended up building that Gilley's Bar. I met this little blond bartender girl. She was cuter than a bug's ear. We ended up kind of becoming boyfriend/girlfriend.

One time, probably after the third or fourth load down there, she said to me, "Jim, I haven't been totally honest with you, so I want to take you over to Lake Worth and introduce you to some of my real friends." I said that would be okay. So, we jumped into her old beater of a car and headed over to Lake Worth.

We pulled up in the front of this old neighborhood bar, and before we got out, she said, "Now, when you go in there, if any of the girls in there try to be mean to you don't be shocked." I thought what is this all about? So, we went in, sat down and ordered a beer. Next thing, a couple of girls over there started giving me the most snake-eyed look. I thought to myself, what is going on here?

After a while I had to use the restroom, but by then she'd told me she liked girls as much as she liked boys. This was kind of foreign to me, so I said, "Which one of those restrooms do I use, the boys or the girls?"

"The boys," she said, "but be on the lookout in case some guy comes in."

When I got back to the table I said, "I think you'd better take me back to my semi." That was the end of that relationship!

$5.00 for a Bushel of Wheat

One time when I was going to College in Manhattan, when Earl Butz was Secretary of Agriculture under Nixon, Mr. Butz came to the University to give a speech. Out of the blue, before he gave his speech, he said, "Do any of you have any wheat to sell? Don't sell it. Put it in storage because the price is going to go up." He said he'd been talking to the Russians, blah, blah, blah, and said basically that he couldn't really divulge any secrets but he wanted to let us all know that they were making a deal with the Russians without actually coming out and saying so.

That summer, I cut my all of my dad's wheat. Afterward, dad came up and told me he was going to sell his wheat on this particular day. "No, dad, don't sell it. The price is going to go up." Dad told me that the banks wanted their money. I said, "Wheat's about $2.50 a bushel right now and it's going to go up. Don't sell it. Wait a while." So, he said he would see if he could hold the banker off for a little while longer. He held onto the wheat.

That was the year I started watching the price of wheat and it seemed every day it would go up about 10 cents a bushel. Finally, it got up to about $3.80 a bushel, and dad couldn't stand it anymore. He just came out and said, "I sold my wheat today. I can't complain. I got about $1.30 more for it than if I'd sold it at harvest." He was a happy camper!

I sold my 1,500 bushel of wheat, too. I'd sell 500 bushels, then wait. Then I'd sell another 500 bushels for a little over $4.00. That winter I went in and sold my last 500 bushels for $5.10 a bushel. That was over 50 years ago. Today a bushel of wheat is worth less now than what I sold wheat for back then. It's a crying shame, isn't it?

My Final Farming Days

I remember the last year of farming, I got my dad to agree to give me a third of the crop since I did all the labor and he furnished the machinery. In the fall of that last year, we had a beautiful stand of milo. It looked like it'd make 100 bushels an acre, which was about three times the normal yield. We were pretty excited about it. Went and cut a sample. It was running about 23 percent moisture, which was a little bit too wet.

I ran into a farmer in town who said he had some dry milo out at the lake area north of town there. Said he'd hire me for two or three days to let our milo dry up a little. So I went out and cut for him for two or three days. On that last evening, I told him, "Well, I'm going to pull out tomorrow and go start cutting our own milo." He said that was fine. I looked to the west. A front was moving in. All of a sudden the wind came up, a cold wind out of the north and it started snowing. That night we got about 12 inches of wet snow. It snapped all the milo over. That wind pushed all those nice heads into the mud. We never were able to even cut most of it. That was the end of that milo crop.

Then I was getting the wheat ground ready. The old 70D tractor was about on its last leg. They wanted $4,000.00 to trade the 70D for a used 4010 John Deere tractor. When the steering rod broke, I just threw up my hands, and I said, "That's it! I can't go on like this anymore. No more, I'm out of here." That was the end of my farming days.

Student Teaching in Burlingame

After four years of college, I dropped out of school to run my dad's semi while he healed up from a heart attack. When he got well enough, I thought to myself, I only have one year of college left. I should just go back and get my degree, so I went back. Of course, the second semester I was enrolled in agricultural education and figured I might become an agricultural school teacher. So the last two months of the semester, it was time to go do some student teaching. I took my little green Volkswagen and headed down to a town called Burlingame, southwest of Topeka. I rented a room from an older lady and thought well, this student teaching ought to be interesting.

After about the first month of student teaching, I was by myself. The regular school teacher said he'd had enough, he couldn't take it anymore. He took off and went back to Minnesota because the school board wouldn't give him a fair salary. The guy was just an excellent school teacher and they only offered a $200 a year raise (from $6,000 to $6,200) after he spent two summers getting his Master's Degree. He wasn't a very happy camper. Luckily, I did the best I could.

After about a month, I'm hiding my chewing tobacco because I didn't want to be a bad influence on those kids. I didn't want them to know I chewed tobacco. I knew all the kids and they knew me and they respected me for being a conscientious teacher. I was already satisfied that if I was going to be a teacher, I was going to be a good teacher because I had some teachers that weren't the best.

So, I left my drawer open after about a month so somebody would notice my can of chewing tobacco if they cared to look. Sure enough, this little junior high school girl came in and looked down in my desk drawer that I had left partially open, and she said, "Mr. Grennan, I didn't know you chewed tobacco."

I said, "Well, I do." It probably wasn't 20 minutes and the whole school knew that Mr. Grennan chewed tobacco. So, well I'm not going try to be deceptive to these kids, because I don't like deception, so I think it was that easy.

I had to stay at that school until probably 9 o'clock, keep the shop open for the kids to come in and work on their projects. That evening that same junior high school girl came in and asked me a question and I answered it. She started to walk away and I looked at her back pocket, and I noticed she had a can of chewing tobacco in her pocket. I hollered at her and I asked, "Hey, Lulu, when did you start chewing tobacco?"

She said, "Mr. Grennan, I've been chewing tobacco since I was about 11 years old." I thought, yeah, right!! Well, maybe she had, and maybe she hadn't, but that was the first time I'd seen chewing tobacco on her.

About two weeks before the end of the school year, one of the teachers came in to my class, asked me if it'd be alright if she put one of the students from the main high school into the shop class. I said, well, yeah, that'll be alright with me. She proceeded to tell me that this boy was a hellion and I would be the teacher who could handle him. He was just a no good hoodlum, and blah, blah, blah. So, that afternoon, he came in and sat down. He had a motorcycle jacket on. I found out later he was an orphan, and that his parents left him off at his grandparents, and didn't want him. I kind of felt sorry for the kid. I asked him if he'd stay after school. He agreed. So I went and had a little talk with him. I said, "You know, we've only got two more weeks of school and I don't want to be here anymore than you do, so why don't we just try to get along and make the best of these last two weeks?"

So anyway, he took a liking to me, because he could tell I really cared about him. He needed somebody that literally cared for him. He asked me if he could bring his motorcycle in and we'd tear that thing down and overhaul it the last weeks of school. I thought, well, I've got to be honest with him, I know not one single thing about overhauling a motorcycle, but told him that he was more than welcome to bring it in, and if there was anything I could help him with, I'd sure try to help him. I just had to tell him right up front that I might not be the best help for that project. So he brought the motorcycle in and he'd ask me a few things and sometimes I could tell him something and other times I couldn't. But he respected me for that.

So, the last day of school, they had what they called "class night", I believe. There was a big dinner and what have you, and so we had to take some tables from the shop over to the main school and he agreed to help me move them over there. He just kind of latched on to me, and I just thought the world of the kid. So I grabbed the table from the front and he got on the back of it and we carried the table across to the main school. There was this little kind of a slew down south of the main school. There was kind of a little foot bridge there with no railing on it. All of a sudden I got on that bridge and felt that table kind of shaking and pretty soon he drops it, lost his balance and went over into the slew. I went back, and asked what had happened?

He said, "I kind of got dizzy and lost my balance."

I looked in his front pocket and he had a pouch of Red Man Chewing Tobacco. I said, "How long have you been chewing tobacco?"

He said, "Oh, Mr. Grennan, I've been chewing tobacco for years." I thought, nah, I don't think so. You only get dizzy maybe the first a week or so, and you quit getting dizzy after that. I thought, man, what an influence I'm having on these kids, and it's not good!

The last day of school they had a big pig roast dinner. I helped serve the pork. I remember serving either burnt pork, pork cooked just right, and some that needed a little more cooking. The fire in the pit was way too hot. When I sat to eat, I was seated next to a hog farmer. If anybody knows anything about raising hogs, you know that hog farmers can take a bath, and take another bath, and they still excrete a smell. I'm not going to say it ruined my dinner, but I kept my mind on why we were all there. I got to thinking years later it was no wonder why the girls at the junior college, when I was going there, didn't want to hang around me. In the afternoon, after I got off of class, I'd go work on a hog farm. Make a little grocery money, basically, and spending money. I thought that it kind of put things in perspective.

All the time in the evenings, when I got out of the shop about 9 o'clock, I'd go by the liquor store and buy a 6-pack of beer. I was so tired from the day's teaching events that I'd just get into my room, pop a beer, guzzle it, pop another and guzzle it, pop another one and guzzle, until I'd guzzled that 6-pack of beer in a matter of no time. I was then able to lay down and go to sleep, get up the next morning, be at the school by 7:00, and needless to say when I got done with my student teaching I came to the conclusion that I wasn't cut out to be a school teacher.

James Grennan

So, I thought maybe I could be a county agent, you know, with a college degree. I didn't want to waste it. So one evening I had an interview over in Lincoln County, Kansas. Went all the way over there, sat down in front of about four old farmers and a couple of town's people. There were pertinent questions, like do I like to go fishing, (I guess because they had a nice little river running through town). There were several other questions, and then finally, one of them said, "Are you the type of person who likes to get up at 3 o'clock in the morning?"

I thought for a minute, and I just said "No, are you?" That was pretty much the end of the interview. They just all closed their notepads and that ended the interview. Nonconformists never seem to catch on to political correctness.

"Even if a farmer intends to loaf, he gets up in time to get an early start." Edgar Watson

Conclusion

After my student teaching was over, I went back home and started driving a truck for my dad again. Something just didn't feel right. When I was headed north in the truck, I wished I was headed south; when I was headed south, I wished I was headed north. I felt like I was wasting my life away, because I realized that there was no future in driving that truck.

Then my brother called, and asked me to come out to Colorado where he was living. He had a job waiting for me at Great Western Sugar. I told my dad that I would like to move out to Colorado and take a chance. He supported that idea, so I loaded up my green VW and headed west to Colorado for my next adventures.

Additional Family Photos

Yard with semi, '51 Ford, and tractor

Grain hauler

Dad's early thrashing machine

Jim's first season; with Cousin Sue Townsdin

Brother Pat as 12 years old helping tarp the load

Load of hay

Combine crew horsing around
L-R: Mike Crum, Bill Kadel and Pat

Dad, Kevin and Ace greasing the one way

John Grennan relaxing in the field

Hooking up the header trailer
L-R: Jim, Charlie Thompson, Brother Pat, Joe Willie Thompson

Dad, Ace, Kevin and Pat getting combine ready for Nebraska

Big Red hauling hay

Ace at 12 years old out plowing on the old D

121

Brother Pat plowing

Kevin cultivating milo

John Grennan standing by his truck

Made in the USA
Monee, IL
07 November 2020